My Godfather's
Italian Fish Tales
Seafood Recipes of Central & Southern Italian Influence

By Donato Fortebraccio

2004

Table of Contents

Dedicated to
Giovanni Coppola

The author in a vineyard of San Giminagno.

Foreward

Cooking Today

Italian recipes have changed and evolved from one generation to another. Italians have intermarried and have thus been influenced by many different ethnic and cultural approaches to cooking. For example, Marie from Canada may have learned how to stuff eggplant from her Italian mother-in-law, but later become a gourmet and added a cream sauce rather than the traditional tomato sauce. Hence, peasant and country fare started to change. You will see these changes in the unique and unusual recipes in this book.

Fifty years ago, you didn't find "Italian Gourmet Fare" on the menu. Contemporary chefs have brought in their *primi piatti, insalate, pasta, secondi piatti* and even their *bevande* with distinct changes in the Italian fare of yesterday. The basic spaghetti and meatball dish is not on the menu today. You will instead find *Salmone alla Griglia con Pure di Patate al Limone e Bietola* (grilled salmon with prepared Meyer lemon whipped potatoes and Swiss chard). Imagine, Swiss chard on the menu!

Housewives and chefs today have visited the Italian hilltops and their cooking reflects the influence of these visits. Many have attended cooking classes in Tuscany. They are using fennel, sage, rosemary, red pepper flakes, basil and wine in their cooking. But when they start cooking rabbit with a Sangiovese sauce or prepare lemon braised calamari with Sicilian olives, roasted heads of garlic with *focaccia* flat bread and gorgonzola cheese, you know that they have evolved into the present day. Yes, the preparations in this book are somewhat gourmet, but still retain a distinct peasant essence.

Donato Fortebraccio

Bruno Marinaro

Introduction

I am a third-generation Italian-American, fascinated with my heritage and passionate about my roots in southern Italy. In 1902 and 1903, my grandparents left Abbruzzi and Calabria and came to this country via Ellis Island. In search of work and a better way of life, they created a particular lifestyle in America incorporating all the Italian customs and traditions, love of family, good food and wine, that reminded them of the old country.

After a mushroom hunt.

I was raised in a household that had a steady stream of relatives visiting not just for the holidays, but many times during the week. They all had stories to tell which they would embellish with facial gestures and body motions worthy of a theatrical production. We always laughed and cried together, gave advice, shared problems and lived life to its fullest.

The men in the family were fishermen and

Mio babbo Giovanni Fortebraccio

hunters of wild game, as they were in Italy. You cannot imagine the stories that came from the kitchens on the day after the hunt. If someone shot a deer, the story would be told endlessly for the coming year or two. If however, the hunt were less successful, they would pick wild mushrooms, borrow a goat or a screaming suckling from a farmer or pick apples in an orchard. They rarely came home empty-handed or without a story to tell. I, too, learned to tell stories at an early age, but also to appreciate good and flavorful food.

My entire family lived in the same neighborhood – upstairs, downstairs, next door, down the street, across Swasey Field or off Broadway. I knew what every aunt was preparing for her family on any given night. If Zia Angela were making homemade fusili with a tuna sauce, I would put her on my list of visits along with Zia Dena, the expert on chicken soup with homemade tagliolini. If Cugino Giovanni had a pepper and egg sandwich for lunch at school, made with Squashy's crusty Italian bread, it was evident in the aroma coming from the bag and the olive oil stains. He always had an extra sub roll in the bag for Donato – no peanut butter

Zio Giovanni Procopio

and jelly sandwiches here! For some reason the Italians all sat together at lunchtime. We shared our love of food, customs and traditions, even at a very young age. We had our own identity; we were Italian Americans and proud of it.

When we sat down for a meal, it was a feast and it was always based on the freshest ingredients that were acquired locally. The tradition of abundant food and storytelling is the heart of this book, ITALIAN FISH TALES. I hope you enjoy the stories and recipes as I have enjoyed writing them. Salute!

The author and his wife gather with friends at Nosdeo's apartment in Rome.

Giovanni Coppola

His Personality Went into his Cooking Vivare

Let me tell you about my godfather Giovanni. He was a man of no mean accomplishment – cook, vintner, butcher, grocery vendor and erstwhile real estate tycoon. He came to this country as a young man from San Pietro di Maida, a small hill town in Calabria, Italy. This was a poor, mountainous seaside region, known for dried pasta, fresh vegetables, fish diets and a crucifix in every room. Meat was reserved for special occasions and it was usually goat; however, every winter a large *maiale* was slaughtered and made into fresh and dried sausages which were stored in the cellar in large crocks filled with olive oil.

When my *compare* arrived in this country via Ellis Island (and that's another story), he went to work in Boston area restaurants, bringing with him the flavors of Italy. His personality reflected his determination to preserve this honest, old-world cooking. His love for and romance with food and his innate knowledge of recipes from his homeland became sought after because he constantly talked about his native land and its classic, distinctive cuisine.

In fact, Italians are always talking nonstop about food and their previous meal. One of these men returned to his *paese* every summer because he had left behind a sum of money and a small farm. He ate and drank so much (to use up the money) that he *scoppio* (burst open) and was buried on the side of the mountain.

My *compare* eventually became a "substantial and highly respected member of the community" according to his friends and neighbors, which is where I came into the picture.

I was very fortunate to join with him in the kitchen and see firsthand his art of cooking. This contact with *Compare* Giovanni became my *vitalizio* in cooking as well as in everyday life. I provided him with rabbit and pheasant from my hunting trips and if I were unlucky in shooting any wild game, I would borrow a young goat from an unsuspecting farmer. This was a trick I learned from my *nonno*. *Compare* Giovanni prepared these gifts for his discriminating friends at the Liberty Club on River Street in Haverill. I learned to play bocce and drink wine mixed with orange soda at this *bastone* and at age seven, I was taller than many of the men there. They were hard working, full-blooded Italians from all parts of Italy who had discriminating and sensitive palates. They were experts of all things culinary. After all, they experienced their mama's and *nonna's* colorful cooking and huge double portions for years. Even after they were married, these men continued to have their ritual Sunday and holiday dinners with their mamas. Many of them lived with their own families in apartments above their parents and every night at dinnertime, a large platter of pasta would arrive at their door. It was like a *miracola*. The pasta would suddenly appear – pasta *ceci*, pasta all'Arrabiata, gnocchi, pasta with clams, pasta with *baccala,* pasta with eggplant, pasta with cabbage, pasta with *polpette* and *salsiccia con pepperoni* – pasta, pasta, pasta. *Ogni giorno. Ogni giorno.* It would be *calamitoso* if you didn't have pasta every day. The Italians have a love affair with pasta and this abundance of food every day of their lives. If a relative or neighbor were *male*, watch out! These short, plump, busty women, always dressed in black with rolled stockings and their hair pulled back in a bun, could be seen charging up the hill into tenements carrying a large kettle of *zuppa*, skillfully blended with an infusion of a dozen vegetables and a *gallina* and of course *pastina al uovo*. These *generale* took command. Often trailing behind would be their short *marito* with a head that looked like a *zucca*, his white stockings showing because his pants were rolled up, carrying in his bag a dozen eggs and a bottle of Moxie, the *cura* of everything. But also in the bag was a small bottle of oil for his *moglie* to use in the anointment of the ill person who may have had an evil eye cast on him. In today's terms, these men would be considered "kept men." Most wives watched over their men, bathed them every Saturday, pressed their underwear, and ironed their sheets. The *moglie* handled all the banking, all legal matters, met her husband at work when he received his pay, gave him an allowance, shopped for the groceries, and was in charge of all events and holidays from baptisms to weddings to funerals to the selection of their sons' wives. She had input in naming the grandchildren, protecting them from reprimand, and deciding appropriate dress codes for all occasions.

I can recall going up to *Compare's* third-floor tenement one Sunday morning (It was a religious experience!) with a bushel of short lobsters for the preparation of Lobster Fra Diavolo. I worked my way up the stairs past cracked and patched walls. There were cans of olive oil, empty jugs of wine, dried oregano, empty ricotta cans, *baccala* (dried codfish) soaking in a chipped white porcelain pan of water, cans of sardines and anchovies in shopping bags in commanding positions on every step. Mingled smells of fresh sweet basil, parsley and garlic came from the porch above. But most prominent was the acrid aroma coming from the empty wine bottles with their residues of wine-

The author and Luigi.

turned-vinegar. If only I could have captured those rich aromas and saved them in a bottle. At the top of the stairs stood *Compare* Giovanni in his stained white apron, a *stogie* in his mouth, a two-day beard and a big grin that revealed his gold tooth. He posed like a *statista* and gave me a big *chiudere gli occhi* out of his crooked left eye. His big battled nose was a deep purple and I knew he was a little *umbriaco*. He always spoke in a very loud voice and until I was much older I thought that was normal. "*Benvenuto,* Donato" he would bellow in his *rumoroso* voice! Now I knew we were ready for some serious cooking, but not until I had a glass of his homemade wine.

This is a long way of getting you to my *compare's* daring and brilliant recipe of "Lobsters of the Devil." Please take the time and try this sensational and intensely flavored recipe. And have a glass of wine before you start. *Salute! Cici!*

Lobster Recipes

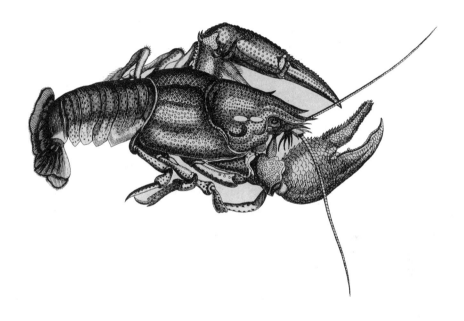

La Pizzo beach, Giovanni and Natalina, 1910.

Giovanni's great great granddaughter Cara enjoying Fra Diavolo.

ARAGOSTA FRA DIAVOLO
(Lobster of the Devil)

Olive Oil   ¼ cup
Garlic   5 cloves, minced
Tomatoes   #10 can, crushed
Lobsters   6, ½ pounds each
Onion   1 very large, finely chopped
Oregano   ¼ Tbsp.
Red Pepper   1 Tbsp.
Cilantro   ½ cup, Italian parsley
Anchovies   3, chopped
Lemon   ½ grated rind
Finocchio(fennel)   5 sprigs
Pernod   1 Tbsp. (optional) in place of fennel
Clam broth   ½ cup (fish stock can also be used)
Vermouth   ½ cup, sweet
Basil   6 fresh leaves, chopped
Linguini   2 or 3 lbs.

Break off the claws, tails and bodies. Remove the black sack beneath the eyes and the vein on the back of the tail. Cook over a low flame in a large skillet with olive oil, onions and garlic. When lobsters have turned red (turning them over a few times for about 5 minutes) then place in a large pot.

Add to the large pot the remaining olive oil, garlic, onions, lobster and its juices. Then, add the remaining ingredients except for the clam broth and vermouth, which should be added after five minutes of gentle stirring. No need to add salt because of the anchovies. Cook covered for 15 minutes over a low flame. The liquor will burn off but a hint of the taste will remain.

Boil 2 to 3 pounds of linguini in salted water until al dente and drain. Place on a large platter and pour prepared sauce on top and mix well with the pasta. Arrange the lobster pieces on top and garnish with basil sprigs. *Mangia, figlio mio!*

Serves 6

During the summers of my youth, I was always at the dock to watch the lobster-men arrive with their catch. They knew what I had in my sack and were eager to swap some lobsters for a bottle of homemade wine. My *compare* Giovanni trained me well in bartering and I would always bring home lobster for a Friday dinner. I never paid for fresh lobster until I was fifty years old!

Lobster can be prepared so many ways as you will note in this *libro*. This particular recipe is simple and tasty because it is enhanced by fennel leaves and fresh lemons. What really gives it a finishing touch, however, is the splash of Sambuca.

ARAGOSTA CON LIMONE E SAMBUCA
(Lobster with Lemon and Sambuca)

Lobsters, Select   6 2-pounders, boiled
Bread crumbs, Italian   ½ cup, flavored
Ritz crackers   4 cups, crushed
Fennel (seeds can be used)   10 leaves, chopped
Olive Oil, extra virgin   ¼ cup
Parsley   2 Tbsp., chopped
Sambuca   ¼ cup
Salt and Pepper to taste

After the lobsters have been boiled, split them lengthwise, being careful not to fracture the shells. Remove the meat and place with the bread crumbs, crackers, fennel, olive oil and parsley in a large bowl. Salt and pepper to taste. Loosely stuff the lobster shells and arrange in a large baking pan. Drizzle Sambuca, lemon juice and butter over the top and bake for 10 minutes in a preheated 375° oven. Check for tenderness.

Serves 6

Next is a recipe given to me by a poor fisherman's wife in Viareggio, Italy on the Versilia Coast (loved by Michaelangelo). This is a true story. When times were lean and tough during World War II, tourists did not frequent this fashionable seaside resort. Fishermen in this region relied on their own catch to survive while people in the nearby mountains made flour from chestnuts for their bread. While the Germans occupied this region, thanks to "Il Duce", the clever fishermen would sneak up to the mountains of Barga and Lucca at night and swap fish for eggs, lard and olive oil. Some of the farmers had goats for milk (if they didn't eat them), and goat's milk can be used for this recipe.

FRITTATA CON ARAGOSTA
(Eggs with Lobster)

Lobster   2 cups, chopped, precooked
Pasta, linguini   ½ lb., precooked
Eggs   1 dozen, medium, beaten
Cream (or goat's milk)   ½ cup
Brandy   ¼ cup, stock
Cheese   ½ cup pecorino, grated
Olive Oil, extra virgin   ¼ cup
Scallions   ½ cup, chopped
Garlic   4 cloves, chopped
Tomato   4 slices, thin
Zucchini Flowers   8 left whole, rinsed
Parsley/Flat leaf   1 Tbsp., chopped
Salt and Pepper to taste

In a large mixing bowl, combine the lobster, cooked pasta, eggs, cream, brandy, and cheese. Add salt and pepper to taste. Blend gently. Meanwhile, in a large oiled skillet, lightly brown the scallions and garlic. Add the lobster mix to the skillet and cook over a low flame for 3 minutes or until lightly browned on the bottom. (Check with a spatula.) Add the tomato slices on top, place the skillet under a broiler and lightly brown the top of the frittata. Place a zucchini flower on top of each serving and sprinkle with oregano and olive oil.

Serves 4

My *compare* was always playing a *scherzo* on his friends. He had a technique of stuffing a potato that was most unique. There was no seam visible in the potato, yet he was able to infuse it with pieces of lobster in a rich cream and brandy sauce.

PATATI SORPRESA CON AROGOSTA
(Surprise Potatoes with Lobster)

Potatoes   6 white, medium
Butter   ¼ lb.
Cream   1 cup, heavy
Egg   1, large
Parsley   1 Tbsp. flakes
Basil   4 leaves, chopped
Garlic Salt or flakes   1 tsp.
Lobster   1 lb.
Flour   ¼ cup
Bread crumbs   ¼ cup
Olive Oil   1 tbsp.
Vinegar   2 tbsps.
Parmesan Cheese   ½ cup, grated
Salt and Pepper to taste

Boil the potatoes until slightly firm. Gently set them aside to cool, being careful not to damage their skins. Once cooled, cut potatoes in half and remove the pulp with a small spoon, keeping the outer shells intact. In a mixing bowl, chop the potatoes, add the melted butter, heavy cream, egg, pulp of potatoes, herbs and spices. With an egg beater, blend the mixture until thick. Add the chopped lobster. Blend. Stuff the potato shells and place together, using the same potato halves to form "whole" potatoes. Roll gently in flour and bread crumbs, concealing the seams and place in oiled baking dish. Cook in preheated 375° oven turning gently for 20 minutes. Place on top of seasoned chicory.

This makes a wonderful appetizer or luncheon entrée.

Serves 6

THE LOBSTER SPECIALIST
Giovanni J. Forte

Mia *babbo* Giovanni, now 93 years old, is a short thin man with a neatly trimmed baffo. He could eat six lobsters at one sitting! Every Friday during the summer months, he had Lobster Diavolo with a pound of *fusili lunghi* and a liter of home-made wine for dinner. And that's no *bugia*. We summered at Salisbury Beach in Massachusetts, where I was a lifeguard, and I would dive for these *creaturi* of the sea on my days off.

Lobsters can actually live a few days out of the ocean, but they must be kept in a refrigerator, stored in plastic bags, preferably with seaweed.

Appropriate timing is very important when cooking lobsters. My father suggests the following:

HARD SHELL (boiled lobsters)

Fill pot ¼ full of salted water.

Lobster Size	Boiling Time
1- 1 ¼ lbs.	10 – 15 minutes
1 ½ - 2 lbs.	15-20 minutes
2 – 3 lbs.	20 – 25 minutes
3 – 6 lbs.	28 – 32 minutes

Giovanni will not bother with lobsters any larger.

HARD SHELL (baked lobsters)

Add 3 minutes to boiling times above for baked stuffed lobsters.

Note: *Mia babbo* told me, "When boiling or baking soft shell lobsters, reduce cooking time by at least 3 to 4 minutes."

STUFFED LOBSTER ALLA DONATO

Lobsters, Maine   6 select, 2 ½ lbs.
Lobster meat   1 cup, cooked and chopped
Scallops, Bay   1 lb., cleaned
Shrimp, Medium   1 lb., uncooked, deveined
Cod   1 cup, blanched
Lemons   3, juice from
Sherry, Sweet   ¼ cup
Ritz crackers   3 cups, crumbled
Parsley, fresh   ¼ cup, chopped
Butter   ½ lb., melted
Salt and Pepper to taste

Prepare the live lobsters by cutting down the stomach through the tail and make a cavity, trying not to cut through the lobster shell. Gently remove the black bag under the eyes, the vein on the back, and set lobsters aside in large sheet pan.

In a large mixing bowl, combine the scallops, shrimp, cod, extra lobster meat, lemon juice, Ritz crackers and sherry with melted butter. Mix thoroughly and stuff the select lobsters. Bake in a pre-heated 375° oven for 15 minutes, or until lobsters are cooked. (Sample a small piece of lobster meat from the tail.)

Need I say more?

Serves 6

Fish Recipes

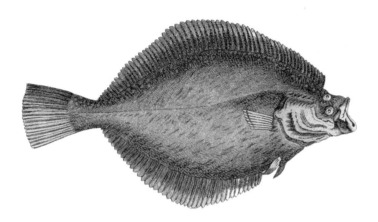

Arlene and Rosetta

Ristorante St. Anthony in Luca.

FLOUNDER STUFFED WITH LOBSTER

Shallots   2, chopped
Garlic   1 clove, chopped
Carrot, cooked   1 medium, finely chopped
Parsley   ¼ cup, chopped
Sweet butter   ¼ lb.
Sherry or Vermouth   ¼ cup, sweet
Lemons   3, juice from
Spinach   ¼ cup, cooked and drained
Lobster meat   1 lb., precooked, chopped
Ritz crackers   1 cup, chopped
Flounder,   2 lbs. large fillets, cleaned
Paprika   ¼ tsp.
Salt and Pepper

In a large skillet, melt the butter and add the shallots, garlic, carrots, parsley and sauté for 5 to 8 minutes. Add the sherry, lemon juice, spinach and lobster meat. Stir well and sauté for only 3 to 4 minutes longer.

In a large mixing bowl, add the crackers and mixture from the skillet. Blend well. On a large platter, place the fish in bread crumbs coating both sides, keeping in mind that flounder is a delicate fish. Spread open and place the mixture evenly on top of fish. Roll up and fasten with toothpicks, carefully placing on a buttered baking pan. Pour additional butter on top of each roll and sprinkle with paprika. Cook in a preheated 375° oven for 10 minutes.

Serves 6

Tuscany's coast is a very attractive place to visit, not only because of its scenery and beaches, but also because of its wonderful restaurants that serve an abundance of fish dishes. On a recent two-week trip starting in Grosseto and continuing north to Forte di Mare, I had an unusual fish meal every day. Here is a fine example.

FARCITO SALMONE CON ARAGOSTA
(Salmon Stuffed with Lobster)

Lobster   1 cup, cooked and shredded
Spinach   1 cup, cooked, chopped and drained
Garlic   1 clove, chopped and sautéed
Onions   2 white, chopped and sautéed
Carrot   1 cooked and diced, sautéed
Fennel   1 stalk, chopped fine and sautéed
Cheese   ¼ cup Parmesan, grated
Egg   1, large beaten
Vermouth   ¼ cup, blended with egg
Bread   toasted, chopped
Salmon   4 medium fillets (skin on 1 side)
Asparagus   1 lb., cleaned with stems removed (to be served with fish)
Butter   3 Tbsp., melted
Paprika   1 Tbsp.
Parsley   1 Tbsp., fresh, chopped
Tomatoes   4, poached
Salt and Pepper

In a large mixing bowl, place the lobster, spinach, sautéed garlic, onions, carrot and fennel. Add the cheese, egg/vermouth, bread, salt and pepper. Mix well and set aside.

Select thick salmon fillets and cut pockets into the sides. Stuff with the lobster/spinach mixture. Set fish in baking pan rubbed with olive oil. Sprinkle fish with olive oil and paprika and bake in a preheated 390° oven for 15 to 20 minutes or until salmon is flaky.

Top with parsley, lemon juice and lemon wedges. Asparagus spears and poached tomatoes make a wonderful accompaniment to this tasty dish.

Serves 4

My godfather's *zio* Cesare was famous for this *specialte piatto*. He used only fresh products and infusions of alluring blends of tasty herbs and exotic spices, which he told me the Arabs, Greeks and Turks brought to Italy when they invaded Calabria centuries ago. If you look at many southern Italians, you will notice an ethnic influence in their coloring and physical features, particularly their noses. Zio Cesare was a man of immense pride and enthusiasm. He looked like an Arab himself, spent a lifetime in the *cucina*, and introduced his nephew Giovanni to this *romanza* of cooking. Zio Cesare, a short man, was standing on a stool stirring the sauce when he died in his early nineties.

Someone said he fell into a huge pot of clam sauce but I don't know how true that is. I do know that he taught his *nipoto* the many recipes of this mysterious region of Italia. It is said today by sailors coming in with their catch of the day, that they still see shadows and a profile of an Arab through the kitchen and hear a noise coming from a large kettle.

The trattoria situated on the docks below St. Pietro was later inherited by my *compare*, but has been closed for a hundred years. I am tempted to reopen it and rename it in memory of Cesare.

SPINOLA IMBOTTIRE ALL'ARAGOSTA
(Striped Bass stuffed with Lobster)

Celery   1 stalk, finely chopped
Garlic   2 cloves, finely chopped
Onion   1 small, finely chopped
Parsley   ½ cup, fresh Italian, chopped
Basil   4 leaves, fresh, chopped
Thyme   4 sprigs
Carrots   1 cup, cooked, diced
Spinach   1 cup, cooked, chopped, drained
Cracker crumbs   3 cups, prefer Ritz type
Capers   ½ cup

Lobster Meat   2 lbs., fresh, cooked
Butter   2 sticks, melted with juice of 1 lemon
Sea Bass   3 lbs. fillets (2 large pieces)
Bread Crumbs, Italian   1 cup
Cognac   ¼ cup

In a large skillet, lightly brown in butter the celery, garlic and onion. Add the parsley, basil, carrots and spinach and sauté for a few additional minutes. Place in a large mixing bowl. When mixture is cool, add the crackers, capers and lobster meat. Mix well. Dredge the outside of the fish in bread crumbs and place the fish in a buttered baking dish.

   Between the sea bass pieces, add the loose stuffing. Pour the cognac cream sauce (see page 115) evenly over the stuffing. Fasten the edges of the 2 pieces of fish together with toothpicks to hold in the stuffing. Baste the fish with cognac, taking a sip for yourself, and place sliced lemon pieces on top of the fish. Bake covered for 15 minutes at 375°. Drizzle with juices from the fish and cognac. Remove cover and cook an additional 15 minutes uncovered. Place the fish on an oval platter with chicken flavored arborito rice. Garnish with lemon slices and thyme sprigs.

Serves 8

The following recipe was influenced by Chef Alex at Alexander's Restaurant in Naples, Florida, which has been in business for over 10 years and is noted for fine American and European cuisine. In my estimation, it is the finest restaurant in Florida. I rate it 5-star. The best of the best. There are unusual pasta creations, local fresh grouper crusted with Macadamia nuts, exquisite pan roasted veal tenderloin with forest fungi and a port wine sauce, seafood risotto with Maine lobster (flown in), scallops, grouper and shrimp sautéed with shallots and white wine, center pork chops sautéed with caramelized apples, cognac and a cream demiglaze, braised lamb shank served with home-style banana mint chutney and sundried cherry sauce, potato crusted salmon served on a bed of leeks with a red zinfandel sauce, crispy roasted duck served with a rich port wine sauce, imported Swedish lingonberries and sweet potato flan, to name just a few of the fabulous entrees.

   If you are in Naples, Florida, by all means have a meal at this restaurant. You will return again and again as my wife and I have for years. Chef Alexander, formerly of Maine, trained at Johnson and Wales College in Rhode Island.

HALIBUT WITH A LOBSTER CREAM SAUCE
OVER PAPPARDELLE

Halibut, fresh   2 lbs., fillet
Eggs   3, beaten
Bread Crumbs, Italian   1 cup
Butter   ¼ lb. unsalted for cooking fish
            additional ¼ lb. for lobster sauce
Parsley   1 Tbsp., chopped
Garlic   1 clove, minced
Shallots   2, medium, finely chopped
Celery   1 stalk, finely chopped
Carrot   1, finely chopped
Spinach   1 cup cooked, drained
Flour   3 Tbsp.
Marsala wine   1 cup
Cream, heavy   ¾ cup
Salt and Pepper   1 tsp. each
Lobster   ½ lb., cooked and flaked

Cut the halibut into 4 even slices. Rinse in cold water and pat dry with paper towels. Dip the fish into the egg batter and coat both sides. Place the bread crumbs in a large flat platter and lay the fish in the bread crumbs, coating both sides well. Melt the butter in a large skillet, add the fish and cook both sides until lightly browned. Plate the fish and pour the heated lobster sauce (recipe below) on top. Sprinkle parsley on top and a sprig of fennel for presentation.

Grilled yellow and green zucchini , eggplant and peppers go well with this dish.

LOBSTER CREAM SAUCE

On a low flame, melt the butter in a sauté pan and add the garlic, shallots, celery, carrot, and lightly brown, stirring often. Add the flour and cook for 15 seconds, again stirring constantly. Add the wine and bring to a slight boil. Add the cream, spinach, cooked chopped lobster, salt and pepper. Turn heat to simmer and stir constantly with a whisk for 5 minutes until you have a smooth sauce. Pour over cooked pappardelle. Place pieces of lobster on top.

Serves 4

My Wife and I recently visited the ancient town of Sicili in the province of Ragusa, Sicily. We were invited to an entertaining lunch at Rosetta Fornice's fifth floor apartment (no elevator) where we dined on her rooftop overlooking the Piazza. Italians have kitchens all over the place—in cellars, garages, under grapevines and on rooftops. Rosetta cooked, danced the Rhumba with me, sang Italian melodies and told stories about her dancing career in Palermo. Her eighty-seven year old boyfriend Mauro, upset with the scenario, kept saying *"Zitto, zitto."*

The meal started with a mussel/saffron soup and a mixed green salad sprinkled with dark green olive oil, pistachios and huge slices of lemons. *Secondo*, homemade pasta (miniature ricotta ravioli) with a fresh tomato sauce covered with fresh basil leaves, grated goat cheese and truffle oil. The main event was pan-seared sole with artichoke hearts, capers and small browned potatoes with splashes of red flakes of pepper. For dessert we indulged in peeled figs, pomegranate, blood oranges and a variety of cheeses. The Sicilian *limoncello* on a dish of lemon sorbet was *delizioso*. Expresso coffee with Sambuca completed the *colazione*. *Saporito*! I ate and drank so much that I fell asleep in the warm Sicilian sun to Carlo Buti's rendition of "Vivare," by guess who?

The author and Rosetta dance the Rhumba.

SOLE RHUMBA ALLA ROSETTA

Sole   3 1-lb. fillets, cleaned
Cornmeal   1 cup
Bread Crumbs, Italian   ¼ cup
Olive Oil   ½ cup (reserve some for garlic & shallots)
Eggs   6, blended
Cheese   ¼ cup pecorino, grated
Spinach   3 cups, cooked, drained
Parsley   ¼ cup, flat Italian, chopped
Basil   10 leaves, julienned
Shallots   2 medium, diced
Garlic   3 cloves, chopped
Anchovies   2 minced
Limoncello (optional)   ¼ glass
Lemons   6 large, quartered
Salt and Pepper to taste

In a large mixing bowl, add all the above ingredients except the fish, cornmeal, bread crumbs and olive oil. The shallots and garlic should be precooked in additional oil.

In a large, flat dish, blend the cornmeal and bread crumbs. Place the fish in the mix and coat both sides.

Pan fry the fish on both sides in olive oil until lightly browned, then place fish on paper towels to absorb oil.

Serve on top of cooked spinach or lettuce.

Serves 6

FILETTI DI SOGLIOLE
(Flounder stuffed with Crab Meat)

Flounder, Sole   2 lbs. large fillets
Parsley   1 Tbsp. flakes
Oregano   1 tsp.
Salt and Pepper to taste
Wine, dry white   ¼ cup
Cognac Sauce (see page 115 for preparation)

Stuffing Mix

Bread Crumbs, Italian   1 cup
Butter   ¼ lb., melted
Spinach   ½ cup, blanched and drained
Crab Meat (or Lobster)   1 cup, drained
Cheese, Parmesan   ½ cup, grated
Egg   1 medium, beaten

Place the pieces of sole in a buttered baking dish. In a mixing bowl, prepare the stuffing and spread the mix on top of each fillet and roll together. Secure with toothpicks. Brush with a mixture of melted butter, white wine and lemon juice. Sprinkle lightly with parsley, oregano, salt and pepper and bake in a preheated 375° oven for 15 minutes. Use a spatula when serving to prevent fish from breaking apart. Pour cognac sauce on top with a sprig of fresh basil. *Mervaviglioso*!

Serves 4

CODFISH/POTATO LOAF

Potatoes   2 lbs., peeled, boiled, riced
Codfish   2 lbs. fillets, skinned
Olive oil, extra virgin   ¼ cup
Salt pork/*pancetta*   1 Tbsp.
Pepper, red   1 large, diced
Onion, white   1 medium, diced
Garlic   3 cloves, minced
Thyme   1 Tbsp., minced
Parsley   ¼ cup, minced
Anchovies   1 mashed fillet
Eggs, extra large   3, beaten
Corn, creamed   ½ cup
Butter   2 Tbsp., melted
Salt and Pepper to taste
Tomato sauce   2 cups, prepared

Boil the peeled potatoes until tender. Rice or mash them and set aside in a large mixing bowl. Boil the codfish for 3 minutes, remove from water and set aside in separate dish. Flake the codfish when it has cooled. Drain well and add to mixing bowl with potatoes.

In a large skillet, sauté the peppers, onion, garlic, thyme, parsley and anchovies in the olive oil with salt pork, over a low flame for at least 5 minutes, stirring frequently. Then place in the mixing bowl with the riced/mashed potatoes. Work in the beaten eggs and mix well, adding the corn, and salt and pepper to taste. Place in a buttered loaf pan and drizzle butter on top. Cook in a preheated oven for 15 minutes. Place on top rack for the last 5 minutes. Remove from oven and cool for 5 minutes. Divide the fish/potato into thick slices and pour Italian tomato sauce on top.

Serves 6

On my annual trips to Italy, there are two places that I always visit. The first one is in the town of Vinci, well known for the Leonardo da Vinci Museum, and the second is Padua which is next to Venice. I go there to meditate and talk with St Anthony. Really, I talk with him and sit next to his tomb and gently rub his marble *bara*. It's the truth: all of my requests have come true. I wear his medals of 18K gold and have his statues and pictures all around my house.

In the town of Vinci, the residents claim that Leonardo was born there and they always invite me to pay tribute to him by drinking wine at the cantina di Leonardo where we discuss his art and inventions. But, let us get back to Padua.

One day in the early fall of 1981, after enjoying a tasty meal of eel, freshly caught from the Brenta River, and a few glasses of wine from the Veneto region, I was sitting next to the tomb of St. Anthony, praying while rubbing my St. Anthony medals on his tomb as usual, and talking *affare* with him. Crutches and pictures adorned the tomb—evidence of the miracles that have taken place here. I was suddenly startled by a crooked hand being firmly placed on my shoulder. An old lady, in her nineties, was attempting to comfort me, assuming there was some type of illness I was trying to overcome with my prayers. I explained to the signora that St. Anthony always brought me good luck and I was asking him to help with a rather substantial business deal I had cooking back in the states. I thought she was going to sock me. "*Disgrazia, disonore, slealta, sacriliegio,*" she shouted in a raging voice. I had to settle her down and didn't know how to do it. I quickly made a sign of the cross and kissed the tomb and attempted to leave. When she saw how sincere I was with Sant Antonio, she said "*Scusa, scusa. Io no normale, vecchia.*" Then, with a turnaround of emotions, she invited me to her apartment which was around the corner from the *chiesa di* St. Anthony. My new friend, Mariuccia, prepared this wonderful meal for me in her small and very old palazzo. She told me that it was handed down through generations from Cardinal Pietro Valier in 1629.

MARIUCCIA'S BACCALA CON SPINACI
(Codfish with Spinach)

Codfish marinade:

Codfish   2 lbs., fillets, fresh
Vermouth, sweet   ½ cup
Olive oil   ¼ cup
Oregano   1 Tbsp.
Garlic   3 cloves, minced
Lemon   1, juice from
Salt and Pepper to taste

Cut codfish into 8 pieces. Place in bowl and marinate in vermouth, olive oil, oregano, garlic, lemon juice, salt and pepper. Refrigerate for 3 hours.

Stuffing :
Olive oil, extra virgin $\frac{1}{2}$ cup (for marinade and coating ramekins)
Spinach   2 cups, blanched and well drained
Onion, white   1 large, chopped fine
Tomatoes, fresh   2 large, sliced and covered with $\frac{1}{2}$ cup Italian bread crumbs
Cheese, Ricotta   1 cup, drained, whipped with 1 egg
Cheese, Parmesan $\frac{1}{2}$ cup, grated

Rub olive oil in 4 individual ramekins and layer each in equal proportions:

Spinach
Chopped onion
Fish
Tomato slices
Dollop of Ricotta cheese/egg blend
Parmesan cheese, 1 tsp.

Start the process over again using two applications of the above. Place in a pre-heated 375° oven for 10 minutes and then add the mozzarella cheese and cook until the cheese coating is brown. We finished the meal with biscotti allo champagne and expresso.

Serves 4

Dried and salt cod in the market.

My Compare Giovanni soaked his *baccala* (dried and salted cod) for a good 24 hours in cold water in a cool place and changed the water at least 3 times. You can purchase this firm and wonderful-tasting fish in your local Italian market; however, I recommend the pre-soaked variety. My compare was an expert at preparing this traditional dish the night before Christmas, *viglia di natale*, with many other fish dishes. It is one of the most *gustoso* sauces I have ever enjoyed.

SALSA CON BACCALA E POMODORO FRESCO
(Salted Codfish with a Fresh Tomato Sauce)

Olive oil, extra virgin $\frac{1}{4}$ cup
Onion   1 medium, chopped
Garlic   3 cloves, chopped
Codfish   2 lbs., salted, pre-soaked, rinsed, drained, in 4-inch pieces, dredged in flour
Olives $\frac{1}{2}$ cup, Italian black
Capers $\frac{1}{4}$ cup, rinsed
Basil   4 fresh leaves, chopped
Oregano $\frac{1}{2}$ tsp.
Parsley   1 Tbsp., Italian, chopped
Bay leaf   1 whole
Fennel   4 pieces outer leaves
Red Pepper $\frac{1}{2}$ tsp., crushed
Tomatoes, ripe   5 lbs., peeled, chopped
Linguini   2 lb.
Salt   (for pasta only)
Wine $\frac{1}{2}$ cup dry white

In a large deep skillet, lightly brown the onion, garlic and codfish in olive oil. Then add all the above, except the wine. After cooking covered for 10 minutes over a medium flame, enrich the sauce with good wine and stir often and gently. An additional 10 minutes of cooking should be *abbastanza*. The codfish is salty, so no need for salt.

Boil the pasta with 1 tsp. of salt and drain. Place in a deep platter with the *baccala* and sauce on top. (See Salsa Subito page 116)

Serves 5-6

Compare Giovanni could always be counted on to prepare a pre-Lenten meal for his friends and family. He never compromised his cooking. Compare used only fresh fish and vegetables, bursting with flavor, enhanced by adding herbs and spices from his garden. All his meals were vibrant and satisfying. He was like a chemist – knowing precisely what and how much flavor he wanted for the correct mix. While he was cooking, he would listen to his favorite Italian tenor, Carlo Buti, belting out "Primo Amore."

Everyone in the neighborhood could smell the wonderful aromas and hear the music coming from his third-floor headquarters high on Maxwell Street, over-looking the Merrimack River in Haverill.

CODFISH CAKES

Codfish   2 lbs., fresh fillets, pre-boiled 2 minutes, shredded
Bread crumbs, Italian   ½ cup, seasoned
Cheese, pecorino or Parmesan   ¼ cup
Flour   ¼ cup
Cornmeal   ¼ cup
Eggs   2, beaten
Red Pepper, sweet   1, finely chopped
Corn, small kernels   ½ cup
Onions, white   2 medium, finely chopped
Parsley   1 Tbsp.
Anchovies   4 fillets, mashed
Olive oil, imported   1 Tbsp. for mix; ¼ cup for frying
Salt   1 tsp.
Pepper   ½ tsp.
Tomato sauce   1 Qt. prepared Italian

In a large bowl, mix the codfish with the bread crumbs, cheese, flour and corn-meal. Add the eggs, sweet red pepper, corn, onions, parsley, anchovies, olive oil, salt and pepper. Mix well and form into patties. Coat the patties with additional cornmeal and let them rest in the refrigerator for 1 hour. Cook patties in olive oil over a medium flame, turning until browned. Place on a dish with a dollop of marinara sauce on top. Or serve over cooked spinach arranged in a nest.

Serves 6

During the fifteenth century, Palermo was one of the important fishing villages in Sicily. Messina Cefalu, Termini and Trapani were also very active. Sea bass and tuna were popular fish and the fasting demands of the church greatly influenced this industry. Fresh and dried fish, eel, salted small tuna and blue fish were eaten instead of meat three to four times a week.

The fishermen lived in a village called Kalsa, a rather poor district of Palermo. When I visited Kalsa, I met a vendor named Alessio who operated a kiosk selling fried eels from the Simeto River near Palermo. I was attracted by the intense aromas that were generated from his elaborate and colorful kiosk. He had a wooden leg, an injury suffered while netting tuna with his seine nets. Thanks for this wonderful recipe, Alessio.

MELANZANE CON BRANZINO
(Eggplant and Sea Bass)

Sea bass   4 4-oz. fillets
Olive oil, extra virgin   2 Tbsp.
Butter   ¼ lb.
Rosemary   5 sprigs
Kosher salt and Pepper to taste
Nutmeg   1 tsp.
Eggplant   1 large, sliced in ½" thick circles
Eggs/milk   2 large beaten with ¼ cup milk; 2 yolks for sauce
Bread crumbs, Italian   ½ cup
Marsala wine   ¼ cup
Lemon   1, juice from
Flour   1 Tbsp.
Cheese, Parmesan   ¼ cup, grated
Ricotta cheese   1 cup, drained
Cream   ½ cup
Fennel   5 sprigs
Swiss cheese, lace   4 thin slices
Spinach   2 cups, precooked, water removed

Rub the fish with olive oil, top with a sprig of rosemary and arrange in an oiled baking dish. Sprinkle lightly with water, cover with tinfoil and place in preheated 375° oven. Poach the sea bass for 5 minutes, remove and lightly sprinkle with kosher salt, nutmeg and set aside. In a large skillet over a medium flame, add the olive oil and butter and fry the cleaned and sliced circles of eggplant that have been dipped in egg wash and bread crumbs on both sides. Lightly brown the eggplant, remove and gently set aside on an oiled broiler pan. Splash wine in the skillet, lemon juice, and incorporate the following slowly, a little at a time: flour,

Parmesan cheese, ricotta cheese, 2 egg yolks, cream and 1 sprig of fennel. Continuously whisk the sauce on a low flame until the cheeses melt and you have a creamy sauce. Set aside.

Plate the above as follows:

  Gently place the circles of breaded eggplant, leaves of basil, salt and pepper in the oiled broiler pan. Place the sea bass on top. Add the Swiss cheese and place under the broiler until cheese has melted. Plate this by placing the fish/eggplant on top of the cooked spinach. Pour the warm cream sauce and drippings on top and decorate with 4 sprigs of fennel.

Serves 4

Bishop Girardo with the author and his wife.

Grouper is used in the following recipe but you can use another type of firm fish such as cod. When buying fish at your local market, ask the attendant if you can smell the fish. If it smells like fish, don't buy it. "Fresh fish doesn't smell and that's it!" my *compare* Giovanni told me. He actually said it another way, but I won't go there. One time, my *compare* Giovanni made the following meal for a local bishop at the Italian Club. The *vescovo* was so impressed that he guaranteed my compare a place next to him in heaven as his personal chef. Bishop Girardo was a good-looking man and liked to *scherzo*. The women in the diocese were very attracted to him. He had a little *fossetta* when he smiled. But suddenly I was told by *compare* Giovanni "He was a *trasferrire* to a *posta* in Georgia." My *compare* certainly had some concerns, because now he believed that he would lose his cooking assignment in heaven with the bishop.

GROUPER CON MANDORIA
(Grouper with Almonds)

Grouper   2 lbs., fresh fillets
Wine, dry white   ¼ cup
Lemon   2 Tbsp. grated rind
Lemon   1, juice from
Flour   ½ cup
Parsley   2 Tbsp., chopped
Garlic   3 cloves, minced
Cheese, Parmesan   ¼ cup, grated
Olive oil, extra virgin   ½ cup
Salt and Pepper to taste

Make diagonal slices on the fish and rub with the wine, lemon juice, salt and pepper. Set aside in refrigerator and chill for 20 minutes, allowing the marinade to soak into the crevices. Meanwhile, place the additional ingredients in a mixing bowl, except for the wine and olive oil. Mix well. Remove the fish and cut into 4 pieces, place into the mix and coat well. Pour the olive oil into a large skillet over a high flame and lightly brown the fish on both sides. Place in a preheated 375° oven and bake for 10 minutes. Place on a platter with paper towels to absorb the oil. Add salt and pepper to taste. This goes well with a salad and French fried potatoes.   Serves 4

My 93 year old father Giovanni.

Smelts are a favorite of my 93-year-old father, Giovanni. He can still eat a few dozen and if there are any left over, he will have them the next day for breakfast with scrambled eggs. He has the appetite of a lion and drinks only Italian brandy. Most of the time, he eats fish and pasta with vegetables. He goes to the local gym three times a week and works out on the treadmill and completes his exercise by lifting weights. He still drives his sports car and goes square dancing on the weekends. *Mio babbo* worked in the shoe shop from the age of 13 until he retired at 51. He has lived very comfortably ever since on his (I don't know what) annuities. I am still trying to find out how he made his money and where he keeps it. He evidently invested his money wisely. He is immaculate and when he leaves his apartment, he is always in a white, starched shirt, tie and sports jacket. He attends all the birthdays, weddings and funerals of family and friends. If I call him at 10 p.m. he is often still out on the town. When I have asked him, "Where do you go so late?" he always avoids the question and says in a very independent way, "None of your affair." He is up at 4 a.m. to start his brisk 2-mile walk and returns to prepare his eggs with herring, black coffee and a shot of brandy. He completes his breakfast ritual with a teaspoonful of cod liver oil. There is not a wrinkle on his face and he is the picture of health. *Mio babbo* boasts about his age by holding up his driver's license that expires in 2008. When he was a young man, he played the violin and also was a Stand-up singer with a 1930's dance band in Boston. Today, he still has a wonderful operatic voice and sings Italian songs at many senior citizen functions and church services.

SMELTS MIO BABBO
(My Father's Smelts)

Smelts   2 lbs., cleaned, de-boned
Cornmeal   ½ cup, yellow
Flour   ¼ cup
Garlic   4 cloves, crushed
Bread crumbs, Italian   ¼ cup, seasoned
Olive oil   1 Tbsp.
Capers   ¼ cup
Tomato   1 medium, chopped
Lemons   3
Salt and Pepper to taste

Fresh smelts are important in this recipe. With kitchen scissors, cut off the heads and tails. Open up the stomachs and remove the innards. Remove the spine which peels out easily. Rinse under cold water. In a large mixing bowl, combine the cornmeal, flour, garlic, and bread crumbs. Place the smelts in the mixture and coat well.

  Place the smelts in an oiled sheet pan and bake in a 375° oven, turning smelts with tongs (once) until golden brown. The smelts will absorb the oil and take on a light brown crispy texture. For presentation, arrange the smelts on lettuce with lemon slices on an oval platter and sprinkle capers and tomatoes on top. Add salt and pepper to taste.

Serves 4

Smelts   24, fresh, de-boned, cleaned
Olive oil   ½ cup
Flour   1 cup, all-purpose
Bread crumbs   ½ cup
Cornmeal   ¼ cup
Cheese, mozzarella   24 thin slices
Filo Pastry   12 sheets, cut in half
Scallions   24 thin strips, julienned
Butter   ¼ lb., melted
Lemons   6 wedges
Sauce   1 cup, tomato, prepared
Garlic   2 cloves, chopped
Onion   1 large white, sliced
Tomato   1 large, diced
Red Pepper   1, diced
Salt and Pepper to taste

Smelts are usually cleaned at your local fish market. Wash them again and gently open the fish and remove the bone. Place the fish on paper towels to dry. In a mixing bowl, place flour, bread crumbs, corn meal and grated cheese. Dredge both sides of the smelts in this mixture and fry in a large skillet until lightly browned. Place on paper towels to absorb excess oil.

   Spread open the Filo dough and cut 6"x 6" pieces. Lightly brush butter on both sides. Roll the smelt, add a piece of scallion, a slice of cheese and a dollop of sauce. (See sauce preparation below.) Roll the dough in a jelly-roll fashion, leaving the tail showing. Bake in a well-oiled baking pan at 375° until the dough is lightly browned. Arrange on a platter with the lemon wedges. This makes a great appetizer.

For the sauce: In a skillet, sauté the garlic, onion, tomato and red pepper over a low flame until cooked. Add to the Filo dough mixture.

Serves 4

Swordfish is featured on the blackboard menus at the entranceway to back alleys in Pizzo, Calabria. This particular recipe was handed down by a cousin who owned a small trattoria on one of the back streets in this seaside village. Giuditta relied on the local fishermen for her customers. It had to be good if these old salts patronized her 6-table establishment, as Giuditta proudly told us. She grew up in a large family with eleven brothers and she studied the art of Calabrian cooking under the *generale*, Filomena, her mother. She prepared the most unusual fish dishes and sauces that were *preminente*! There are restaurants and there are trattorias in Italy, but Giuditta's was the best of the best. Here is one of her unforgettable recipes. (In later years, she moved to America with her husband Giovanni and is still cooking her *meraviglioso* meals in Utica, New York.)

PESCESPADA ALLA GIUDITTA
(Judy's Swordfish)

Swordfish   4 thick steaks
Bread crumbs/Flour mixture   ½ cup each, Italian crumbs
Olive oil, extra virgin   ½ cup
Eggs   3 large, beaten
Eggplant   1 large, sliced in circles
Tomato   1 cup
Tomatoes   2 cups fresh, stewed
Garlic   3 cloves, minced
Onion   1 medium, minced
Carrots   1 medium, finely chopped
Pepper   ½ green, chopped
Basil   8 leaves, whole
Parsley   4 sprigs, chopped
Wine, dry white   ½ cup
Cheese, Parmesan   ¼ cup
Cheese, mozzarella   4 slices
Squid   4 tentacles, boiled 5 minutes
Salt and Pepper to taste

Dip the swordfish steaks into beaten eggs, both sides, and then dredge in flower and Italian bread crumbs, both sides. Fry in olive oil until lightly browned and semi-cooked. Cut out middle of swordfish with large cookie cutter or large mouthed glass to create a circle of at least 4 inches in diameter. Place in oiled baking dish, saving outer edges of swordfish. Do the same with sliced circles of eggplant (dipping and browning in oil) until lightly browned. Place on top of swordfish cutout. Then do the same with slices of tomato and circles of cheese on top of the pile.

In the same frying pan, add some oil and lightly sauté the garlic, onion, pepper, carrots, basil, and parsley. Add the wine, stewed tomatoes, remnant pieces of swordfish cutouts (crumbled) and squid tentacles. Cook 5 minutes over a low flame. Stir a few times while adding the Parmesan cheese, salt and pepper. Pour over the stacked fish assembly. Bake in a preheated 375° oven for 10 minutes, or until cheese starts to melt. Serve on top of buttered peas and rice. Present with sprigs of basil on top.

Serves 4

Fresh swordfish

My *compare* Giovanni had a back yard that was completely occupied with a vegetable garden. He kept large barrels filled with water-soaked chicken manure and ladled the water mix around the plants. His friends would come to visit and admire his garden – probably an excuse to be invited to taste his homemade wine.

They all left, a little dizzy from the grape juice, with a bag of vegetables under their arms. There were tomatoes, zucchini, pole beans, fava beans, basil, parsley, onions, garlic and more. But what really stood out were the glistening purple eggplants that could be prepared so many ways. You can stuff them with tuna, roll them with cheese inside, fry them in olive oil, use them in tomato sauce, on top of pizza, etc.

Here is one recipe with salmon pancakes that I am sure you will enjoy.

FRITELLE DI SALMONE CON MELANZANE
(Salmon Pancakes with Eggplant)

Garlic   3 cloves, minced
Onions   1 large, white, chopped
Olive oil $\frac{1}{2}$ cup (reserve some for eggplant)
Salmon   1 lb., poached, chopped fine
Basil   5 leaves, fresh, chopped
Parsley   5 sprigs, Italian flat, chopped
Tomatoe sauce prepared   1 pt.
Cheese, mozzarella   4 slices, $\frac{1}{4}$ inch
Bread crumbs, Italian   1 cup ($\frac{1}{4}$ cup for eggplant)
Eggs   2 raw, beaten
Flour $\frac{1}{2}$ cup
Eggplant   4 slices, breaded and precooked (see below)
Salt and Pepper to taste

In a small skillet, lightly brown the garlic and onions in olive oil, reserving some oil for cooking the pancakes and eggplant. Place in large mixing bowl with the salmon. Add the basil, parsley, cheese, bread crumbs and beaten eggs. Slowly add the flour, mix well and shape into small pancakes. As a final step, work both sides of pancakes in flour mixed with bread crumbs.

   In a large skillet, heat the olive oil and fry the salmon cakes until lightly browned on both sides. Place them in a buttered baking dish and top each with eggplant, 2 Tbsp. prepared tomato sauce and 1 slice of mozzarella cheese. Bake for 10 minutes in a pre-heated 375° oven.

Prepare the eggplant:
   Slice a small eggplant into half dollar shaped slices and dredge in Italian bread crumbs mixed with Parmesan cheese. Fry in olive oil over a medium flame until lightly browned on both sides.

Serves 3 or 4

SGOMBRO E VINO BIANCO
(Baked Mackerel in White Wine)

Mackerel   4 medium, prepared for cooking
Lemons   2, juice from
Potatoes   4 medium, white, skins on, cut up
Parsley   4 sprigs, chopped
Celery   2 stalks, chopped
Olives, black   1 cup
Tomatoes   1 cup, crushed
Onions   2 medium, chopped
Garlic   3 cloves, minced
Basil   4 leaves, chopped
Olive oil   1 Tbsp.
Wine, white   ½ cp
Salt and Pepper to taste

Clean and prepare the mackerel by removing the tail, head and intestines. Rub the mackerel with salt and lemon juice. Place in a deep baking dish with cut up potatoes, parsley, celery, olives, tomatoes, onions, garlic, salt and pepper. Drizzle wine and oil on top. Bake in a pre-heated 375° oven for 30 minutes.

Serves 4

When I visit the Forte di Marmi area of Italy, I will often fish in the ocean inlet for salt water eels. This area of Italy is also famous for many other types of fish like sea bass, sole, squid, octopus, tuna and a variety of shellfish. The mussels in this area of La Spegia are very large and are prepared in a garlic based tomato sauce. In this recipe, I have worked the mussels in with the eels, a few pieces of cod and a dozen jumbo shrimp.

ANGUILLA ALL SALSA E ZAFFERANO
(Eels with Tomato Sauce and Saffron)

Eels   2 lbs., skinned, cleaned
Flour   1 cup, all purpose
Olive oil, extra virgin   ½ cup
Onions   2 large white, chopped
Garlic   6 cloves, chopped
Fennel   2 stalks, chopped
Rosemary   3 sprigs
Bay leaf   3 leaves
Parsley   3 sprigs, chopped
Red Pepper flakes   2 Tbsp., crushed
Saffron   2 threads
Tomatoes   6 fresh, diced
Truffle oil   2 Tbsp., pure
Lemon   2, juice from
Marsala wine   1 cup
Codfish or Sea bass   2 lbs. fresh fillets
Shrimp   1 dozen, jumbo, heads on
Mussels   2 qt., brushed and rinsed

To prepare the eels, chop off the heads and tails. Place the eels in a pot with enough water to cover. Bring to a boil for 2 minutes and quickly remove and rinse with cold water. Use a pair of pliers and remove the skin and discard. Chop the eel into 3-inch pieces. Dry on paper towels. Then dredge the eels in flour and set aside. Meanwhile, sauté the onion, garlic, fennel and remaining herbs and spices in olive oil over a low flame, adding truffle oil, tomatoes and red pepper. Cook for about 10 minutes. Add the Marsala, the fish and mussels and cook, covered, over a very low flame for another 15 minutes. Stir the fish sauce often but gently. Set up a sieve over a large pot and strain the fish sauce for about 5 minutes. Gently remove the fish and mussels and set aside. Arrange the fish in individual soup bowls and ladle warm sauce/soup on top.

Serves 6

The author with Captain Rocco.

One day, my *compare* came by my house to take me to the docks where the tuna fishermen came in with their catch. It was a dual treat—he let me drive his closed-in panel truck and I had a chance to go on his cousin Rocco's boat. It was during the war and gas was scarce, so to conserve fuel, I turned off the engine when going down steep hills as instructed. There I was, 13 years old, driving a stick shift truck with a Camel cigarette in my mouth. The gears were grinding and the truck was swerving all over the road. This didn't bother *compare* Giovani at all. He was taking a shot of brandy because, as he would say, "I'm a getting a cold." We arrived at the dock just in time for the boat's arrival. His *cugino*, the captain of the run-down boat, helped us move large tuna to the rear of the truck. I could see my *compare's* eyes light up with dollar signs: 500 pounds of cut up tuna, peddled in the Italian neighborhood of Boston, would fetch him a tidy sum. Of course, we kept the head and removed the jowls for our own consumption.

Here is compare Giovanni's recipe with tuna and cannellini beans. No, we are not using the head in this recipe!

TONNO CON FAGIOLI, POMODORO E FARFALLE
(Tuna with Beans, Tomatoes and Butterfly Pasta)

Tuna steaks   2 lbs fresh, cut into 4 pieces
Flour   ½ cup
Olive oil, extra virgin   ½ cup
Oregano   ½ tsp.
Parsley   3 sprigs, chopped
Basil   3 fresh leaves, chopped
Wine, dry white   ½ cup
Garlic   2 cloves, chopped
Onion   1 medium, chopped
Tomatoes   3 lbs. fresh, crushed
Beans, cannellini   2 cups, cooked
Farfalle   1 lb. (sometimes called butterfly or bow ties)
Salt and Pepper to taste

In a bowl, marinate the tuna in olive oil, (reserving some for the skillet), oregano, parsley, basil, salt, pepper and wine. Set aside in refrigerator for 3 hours, turning it over once.

In a large, deep skillet, brown the onion and garlic over a low flame. Dredge the tuna with flour and add to skillet, browning on both sides. Add marinade, tomatoes and cooked beans to the skillet and cook for 10 minutes over a low flame, stirring lightly.

Pour sauce over farfalle pasta which has been cooked al dente, making sure tuna slices are on top. Garnish with a few sprigs of basil. Add salt and pepper to taste.

Serves 4

PASTRY ROLL STUFFED WITH FISH

Butter   2 Tbsp.
Spinach   1 cup, cooked and drained well
Mushrooms   1 cup, chopped and precooked
Garlic   3 cloves, chopped
Scallions   4 sticks, chopped
Goat Cheese   ½ cup
Parmesan cheese   ¼ cup, grated
Nutmeg   ½ tsp.
Parsley, Fresh   1 Tbsp., chopped
Salt and Pepper
Eggs, fresh   2 large
Flour   ½ cup
Cream, heavy   ½ cup
Fish, fresh   1 lb. fillet of cod, boiled and shredded
Lobster, fresh   1 lb., precooked, chopped
Puff paste dough   1 lb.

In a large skillet, melt the butter and sauté the spinach, mushrooms, garlic and scallions. Place in a large mixing bowl, add the ricotta and Parmesan cheeses, nutmeg, parsley, salt and pepper. In a separate dish, blend the eggs, flour and heavy cream, making sure there are no lumps and add to the mixing bowl. Add the cooked fish, chopped lobster and mix very well. Spread the puff pastry on a buttered baking pan and fill with the prepared mixture. Roll in jellyroll fashion, sealing the edges. Brush with melted butter and place in a preheated 375° oven. Cook for 30 minutes.

Serves 6

The following recipe is for a very refreshing meal to serve during the summer months. It is easy to prepare ahead for guests. You can use fresh tuna or white canned tuna along with other prepared fish. It is really fun to present this colorful dish. Your guests will say "Wow!"

Author's granddaughter Christina with antipasto.

FRESH FISH ANTIPASTO

Lettuce, Boston (Bibb)   3 heads
Tuna   2 cups, chopped
Shrimp   12 medium, cooked
Squid   2 cups, sliced in circles
Clams   3 cups whole, cooked
Capers   ½ cup
Eggs   6 hardboiled, sliced
Mushrooms   2 cups, small, pickled
Cheese, Parmesan   ¼ cup, grated
Cheese, mozzarella   12 small balls
Olives   1 cup green
Beans   1 cup cannellini
Peas   ½ cup, frozen
Corn   ½ cup kernel
Scallions   2 cups, chopped
Tomatoes   6 large, sliced
Parsley   8 fresh sprigs, chopped
Sweet bay leaf   8 whole
Onion   1 red, sliced
Peppers, yellow/red   2 each, sliced thin

Zucchini   1 yellow; 1 green
Zucchini flowers   6 flowers, cleaned
Anchovies   1 small can in oil
Sardines   1 small can
Celery   2 stalks, sliced
Fennel   1 stalk, sliced
Cucumber   1 large, sliced
Olive oil, extra virgin   ½ cup
Vinegar, balsamic   ¼ cup
Croutons, seasoned   1 cup
Lemon wedges, 8 for the side
Salt and Pepper to taste

Present this salad on a large oval platter. Serve with fresh Italian garlic bread. Start the dish with the Bibb lettuce first; then, let your imagination run away with itself. Sprinkle with olive oil and vinegar when the arrangement is complete. My compare Giovanni would also roll some Genoa salami, capacola and prosciutto on the edge of the platter.

   I consider this antipasto a meal in itself. Serve with cold, crisp, dry white wine.

Serves 6

Shellfish, Calamari, & Snails

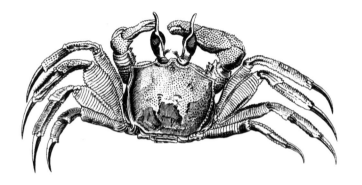

Following is one of the most delicious meals I have ever prepared. Having been raised in the summers by the shore, I have tried every type of fish that comes out of the Atlantic Ocean. My favorites are crab and lobster. You can use either in this easy-to-prepare dish. I have also added uncooked sea scallops to the sauce. I prepared this dish once for my uncle Alfredo and he was amazed with the hint of Marsala and fennel in this delicate sauce. Probably I should have named this sauce after my Uncle Alfredo. Hmmm.

GRANCHIO CON SALSA DI CREMA
(Crab with Cream Sauce)

Cream   1 qt., heavy
Butter   ¼ lb.
Cheese, Parmesan   1 cup, grated
Parsley   ¼ cup, chopped
Fennel   2 sprigs, chopped or 2 tsp. seed, crushed
Basil   6 leaves, chopped
Crab   1 lb. crabmeat pieces, fresh
Marsala wine   ¼ cup
Salt and Pepper to taste
Pasta   1 lb. rigatoni

Pour cream into a large skillet with high sides and stir over low flame. Add the butter and blend with a whisk. Add the cheese, parsley, fennel, crab, Marsala and continue to blend. Add salt and pepper to taste. When the cheese has melted into the mix, about 10 minutes, the sauce is complete.

Meanwhile, boil the rigatoni in salted water until al dente. Drain well and add the pasta to the skillet, mixing well. Turn onto large platter and sprinkle on top the basil and more grated cheese and pepper.

Serves 4

FUNGI IMBOTTITI
(Mushrooms stuffed with Crab Meat)

Bread Crumbs, Italian   1 cup
Crab Meat   1 cup, cooked
Parsley   ¼ flakes
Cheese, Parmesan   ¼ cup, grated
Egg   1 beaten
Olive Oil   ¼ cup
Mushrooms   16 large, uncooked
Butter   ¼ lb. for greasing pan and melting in mix

In a medium-sized bowl, combine bread crumbs, crab meat, parsley, cheese and egg. Work in the olive oil until moist. Mix well. Stuff each mushroom after removing stems and place in baking pan. Pour melted butter on top of the mushrooms as they are cooking. Bake in 375° oven for 10 or 12 minutes.

Serves 3 to 4 as a side dish

The author with vocalist Nosdeo.

When I go to Italy each year, I live on a diet of fresh fish, particularly calamari with pasta. You can find calamari most anywhere you go in Italy whether you are on the highest Tuscan hill or below the boot in Reggio Calabria. In fact, I am told by one of the fishermen in Viareggio that the Papa has it every Friday with taglialini, and his dog, who understands Italian, eats calamari, too.

CALAMARI CON SALSA POMODORO
(Calamari with Tomato Sauce)

Olive oil, extra virgin   ¼ cup
Onion   1 large white
Garlic   3 cloves, minced
Squid (calamari)   3 lbs., cleaned
Basil   5 leaves, chopped
Parsley   5 sprigs, fresh, chopped
Oregano   ½ tsp.
Red Pepper   1 tsp., crushed
Tomatoes   3 lbs., ripe, crushed
Vermouth   ½ cup, sweet
Salt to taste

In a large sauce pan, lightly brown the onions and garlic in olive oil. Add the squid and cook, covered, for about 10 minutes. It is important not to overcook the squid or it will get tough and chewy. Add the remaining ingredients and cook for an additional 10 or 15 minutes, stirring often. Check for tenderness. In a large bowl, pour the calamari and sauce over 2 lbs. of linguini. Now you are ready for the *benedizione*.

Serves 6

My *cugino* Nosdeo's fifth floor apartment in Rome was the scene of a spettacoloso dinner prepared by his son-in-law, Pino. A well-known chef in Rome, Pino combines porcini mushrooms with fish in a cream sauce.

The view from Nosdeo's apartment is breathtaking, with two kitchens, five marble bathrooms, and hand painted fresco ceilings in the huge dining room that seats forty people.

Nosdeo left San Pietro a Maida in Calabria fifty years ago for Rome, to study voice lessons. Unfortunately, the voice lessons were unsuccessful. To survive, he made a living working the streets of Rome with a pushcart selling ladies' underwear. He saved his money, lived a frugal life eating pasta fagioli and invested his savings in land on the outskirts of Rome. Today, he is a very respected, successful businessman who has many apartment buildings throughout Rome.

PINO'S FETTUCINI WITH SCALLOPS, SHRIMP AND HALIBUT IN A CREAM SAUCE

Onion   1 large, chopped
Garlic   4 cloves, chopped
Mushrooms, Porcini   large, sliced
Olive oil, extra virgin   2 Tbsp.
Butter   ¼ lb.
Cream   1 ½ cups, heavy
Milk   ½ cup
Marsala wine   ¼ cup
Cheese, Parmesan   ½ cup, grated
Fontina cheese   ½ cup, sliced
Swiss Lace   ½ cup, sliced
Parsley   3 Tbsp., fresh, chopped
Sea Scallops   2 lbs., cleaned
Shrimp, jumbo   2 lb., cleaned, deveined, pre-cooked
Halibut   1 lb., cubed
Fettucini   2 lb.
Salt and Pepper to taste

In a large skillet, sauté the onion, garlic and mushrooms in oil and butter until lightly browned or tender.

Blend in the cream, milk, Marsala, cheeses and parsley. Add the scallops, cooked shrimp and halibut. Cook for 10 minutes over a low flame, stirring constantly. Meanwhile, boil the fettucini, adding 1 tsp. salt to boiling water, until al dente. Drain well. In a large bowl, place the pasta with the cheese/fish sauce on top.

Serves 8

The author with Chef Pino.

SCALLOPS/MELON WRAPPED WITH PROCIUTTO

Sea Scallops, large   2 lbs., rinsed clean
Marsala wine   ½ cup
Bread crumbs, Italian   1 cup
Butter   2 tbsp.
Olive oil   1 tbsp.
Lemons   2, juiced
Prociutto, imported   1 lb., paper thin
Melon   2 cups, balls
Cherries, pitted   Maraschino
Romaine lettuce   wash and dry
Toothpicks

Soak scallops in Marsala wine for 30 minutes, remove and roll in bread crumbs. Place in skillet and sauté in butter and olive oil over a medium flame, turning over until both sides are lightly browned for a maximum of 3 minutes. Splash with lemon juice.

   Remove scallops and wrap in veils of prociutto, skewer them and bake in a preheated 375° oven for 3 minutes. Remove from oven, skewer the scallops with fresh melon balls and cherries. Great as an appetizer.

Serves 6

The author in a prociutto factory with Mario.
Franco Di Soto, Pisa.

59

SHRIMP WITH BABY ARTICHOKES

Artichokes   4-5 per serving
Lemons   2, juice from
Water   2 cups
Olive oil, extra virgin   ½ cup
Butter   ¼ lb.
Truffle oil (optional)   1 teaspoon
Shallots   6, diced
Garlic   4 large cloves, diced
Wine, white   ¼ cup
Shrimp, jumbo   4-5 per serving, de-veined, precooked
Pasta, linguini   2 lbs., boiled al dente
Salt and Pepper to taste

Prepare the artichokes by peeling the stem slightly and remove the petals until you come to the yellow petals. Cut off the top of the artichoke and its points. Rinse well and place in a bowl with 3 Tbsps. lemon juice and water for 10 minutes. Then place in a large pan with 2 cups of water and steam for 10 minutes, reserving the liquid in a large skillet. Drain the artichokes well. Add to the skillet the oil, butter, truffle oil, shallots, garlic, lemon juice and wine. Add salt and pepper to taste. Cook over a low flame for 10 more minutes and add the artichokes, shrimp, and pasta. Cook another 5 minutes.

Serves 4

Pisa is famous not only for the leaning tower, but also for its many fish restaurants. Like Viareggio and Livorno, Pisa has many fishermen providing a variety of fresh fish daily to these kitchens.

GAMBERO ALLA PISA
(Shrimp of Pisa)

Shrimp   12 jumbo, cleaned, shelled, pre-soaked in 1 cup white wine for 1 hour
Cornmeal   1 cup
Flour   ½ cup
Parsley   ½ cup flat leaf, chopped
Garlic   ¼ cup, minced
Cheese, Parmesan   ¼ cup, grated
Olive oil, extra virgin   ½ cup
Tomato Sauce   1 cup, prepared
Lemons   4, quartered
Salt and Pepper to taste
Skewers   12 thin, 6 inches long

In a mixing bowl, place the above ingredients except for the oil, shrimp and sauce and mix well. Place the de-veined shrimp into the mixture and coat. Meanwhile, in a deep skillet, heat the olive oil over a medium flame. Skewer the shrimp and place in skillet, lightly browning both sides. Place on paper towels and pat dry to remove excess oil. Arrange the skewered shrimp on lettuce with tomato sauce for dipping. Garnish dish with quartered lemon wedges dipped in parsley.

Serves 4 for an appetizer or lunch with a salad.

GAMBERI CON POMODORO E ACCIUGHE
(Shrimp with Tomato Sauce and Anchovy)

Garlic   3 cloves, mashed
Onion   1 large, minced
Anchovy   2, chopped
Finnocchio   4 stalks, chopped (anise flavored celery)
Olive oil, extra virgin   ¼ cup
Tomatoes   3 lbs., fresh, stewed and sieved
Basil   5 leaves, chopped
Parsley   4 sprigs, cilantro, chopped
Oregano   ½ tsp.
Red Pepper   ½ tsp. crushed
Sambuca   ¼ cup
Shrimp   2 lbs., large size, cleaned and deveined
Spaghetti   1 lb., salted

In a large, deep skillet, lightly brown the garlic, onion, anchovy and celery in olive oil for 2 or 3 minutes. Add the tomatoes, herbs and spices. On a low flame, cook for 15 minutes until all the flavors have blended. Add the Sambuca and shrimp and cook for 10 minutes, stirring frequently. Serve on top of spaghetti.

Serves 4

VONGOLI CON SALSA
(Clam Sauce)

Clams, whole   3lbs. cleaned
Olive oil, extra virgin $\frac{1}{4}$ cup
Garlic   2 cloves, minced
Parsley   3 sprigs, chopped
Basil   5 fresh leaves, chopped
Red Pepper $\frac{1}{2}$ tsp., crushed
Tomatoes   1 large can (35 oz.)
Vermouth $\frac{1}{4}$ cup, sweet
Linguini   1 lb.
Salt to taste

In a deep skillet, lightly sauté the garlic, parsley and basil. Add crushed pepper, tomatoes, reserving clams and vermouth. Cook covered over low flame for 20 minutes, stirring often. Add the clams, the vermouth, and cook on medium heat for 5 minutes without cover. Stir. Meanwhile, cook the linguini in boiling salted water until al dente. Strain and place in the large skillet with clam sauce.

Serves 4

VONGOLI CALABRESE
(Steamed Clams)

Clams, in shell, 10 lbs. brushed and cleaned, sand removed. Place clams in a large pot and sprinkle with corn meal, cover and refrigerate for 2 days. Clams will release sand in shell. Rinse and flush thoroughly.

Wine, dry white   1 cup
Onions   2 large, whole
Parsley   6 sprigs, whole
Garlic   3 cloves, whole
Water   1 qt.
Lemon   1, juice from
Butter   ¼ stick, sliced
Salt and Pepper to taste

In a large pot, add the above ingredients, except the clams, and bring to a boil. Lower the flame to medium and add the clams. In about 15 minutes, clams will open. Pour some of the hot broth into 6 individual cups, adding a pat of butter. Then add salt and pepper. Rinse each clam in broth before eating.

Serves 6

The author as a boy.

My godfather was a showman when he cooked. His eyes would tell you a story. If he added too much red pepper, his eyes would go up and he would say, "*Dio!*" If he didn't like a particular taste, his nose would get distorted. He had a style of cooking that was very *dissimile*. He knew what to do at the right time. He constantly tasted his food as he cooked and took a drink of wine as well. His kitchen had all the correct cooking utensils, pots and pans and fresh spices and herbs hanging within reach. The tomatoes were always fresh from the garden or jarred at the farm in the fall. Every Italian had a garden and a grapevine in his back yard or up the hill, nearby. They also had fig trees which they buried in the ground when winter came.

Compare Giovanni's small farm was used on weekends as his *ritirarsi*. It was a meeting place in the summer and fall for his cronies to play bocce, drink their wine, tell stories and smoke their *stogie*. The kitchen at the farm was well equipped and had electricity and well water. Wine was often chilled by being tied to a rope and lowered into the well. The chipped dishes were odds and ends given out by the local movie theater. One of my favorite places to sit was at the large picnic table under the cool grapevine where I might see a young goat turning on the spit. These were very happy summer days during my youth and I was always eager to go to the farm. I was fascinated with the old-timers and their funny gestures and facial expressions that reflected their appetite for life. I will never forget it. There was Antonio, Rolando, Nicolo, Giuseppe, Andrea, Mauro, Siriano, Mario, Francisco, Donato, Bruno, Guido, Alfredo, Rome, Ernesto, Sabatino, Guilio, Ruggero and Danielle — all characters in so many ways. They had red noses and nicknames such as *nasone grande* (large nose), *parla la sempre* (always talking), *coniglio* (rabbit), and *straccio* (rags). Wow, could they eat and drink! They all made homemade wine and argued with each other about who made the best.

My godfather cooked everything imaginable — goat (including stuffed heads), rabbit, woodchuck, raccoon, deer, blackbirds, chicken feet, beef hearts, tripe, suckling pigs, lamb brains, sausages, octopus, squid, eels, and the snails I am presenting below.

LUMACHE CON SALSA
(Snails with Tomato Sauce)

Snails   2 lbs., cleaned; soaked in cold salted water 2 hours
Garlic   2 cloves, chopped
Onion   1 large, sliced
Parsley, Italian   4 sprigs, chopped
Celery   1 stalk chopped
Basil   4 leaves, chopped
Tomatoes   3 lbs., crushed
Marsala wine   ½ cup (could use dry sherry)
Linguini   2 lbs.

Place the fresh snails in a large pot of cold water. Coat the edge of the water with salt to stop the snails from leaving. Soak for 2 hours, changing water twice. Remove and rinse a few times. In a large, deep skillet, place the garlic, onion, parsley, celery and basil and sauté for 10 minutes over a low flame. Add tomatoes and cook covered, for an additional 15 minutes, stirring occasionally. Add the snails, salt and pepper. Add the Marsala or sherry. Cover and cook over a low flame for 15 more minutes, stirring often. Pour over cooked linguini. Use a small pick to remove the snails. *Delizioso*!

Serves 4

Signor Pistolesi

One of the most wonderful meals that I have had in Italy was on the shores of the Ligurian coast of Rapallo. On our way to Monti Carlo, we were invited for lunch by my wife's distant cousin, Mauro Pistolesi. He lived high on a hill overlooking the beautiful and spectacular coastline of this famous port. His grandmother had left him this villa with the understanding that it would stay in the family for generations to come. Italians are noted for leaving property with the stipulation that it never be sold. Another cousin who passed on, left a fig tree and money to maintain it. I was told that this was the way people liked to be remembered.

Mauro was a bank official with many shares in the bank, thanks to his *nonna*. At the age of eighty-nine, Mauro had never married and had no heirs, but for cousins like my wife and me. We had not heard from *Cugino* Mauro for many years and were rather surprised by the invitation. Since we were on our way to France, the reunion worked out well for us. Mauro was always fond of my wife, probably because she talked Tuscan so well and he knew of her passion for Italy and her kindness to his mother. In the late fifties, my wife had spent the summer at the villa. Mauro's mother, Delia, always communicated by mail and telephone from Italy and developed a very close bond that lasted for over forty years. When she passed away, she left my wife some outstanding gold jewelry (which belonged at the Vatican) that had been passed down for generations. Delia had only one son.

We were unaware what we were in for that *splendido giorno*. We were greeted at the gates to the villa by Caterina, Mauro's Sicilian maid who had been with the family for years. She kept house for him and was an excellent cook. We went upstairs to the balcony where Mauro was sitting in a rather large rocker with a *coperta* over his legs. It appeared that he had suffered a stroke, for he talked in a slurred voice from one side of his mouth. I immediately knew something was wrong – particularly when Caterina motioned to us with her large brown eyes upwards toward heaven. Next to him was a large and very old leather box with official looking papers sticking out from the sides. My wife and I embraced him because we knew that this might be a final *incontro*.

Mauro was so happy to see us. He motioned for us to sit next to him and he talked quietly about his state of affairs. Caterina left the balcony to return with some expresso and biscotti. Mauro continued to mumble about the papers in the box and how his mother was very *appassionato* of my wife. Suddenly, he lifted the box and handed it to my wife and asked her to look at the stack of legal papers. Her name was on the front of all the documents and it appeared that she was the heir-to-be. It was a very emotional scene and both Mauro and my wife cried and embraced each other.

Once everything settled down, Caterina invited us into the dining room for the following classic Sicilian meal.

67

GAMBERONI E FINOCCHIO
(Jumbo Shrimp and Fennel)

Olive oil   ¼ cup
Leeks   1 cup, chopped
Fennel   2 stalks, chopped and boiled
Sambuca   2 tsp.
Saffron   3 threads
Raisins   ¼ cup, extra large
Pine nuts   ¼ cup
Shrimp, jumbo   2 lbs., shelled and deveined
Pasta, large rigatoni   1 lb.
Red Pepper   1 Tbsp., crushed

Heat the olive oil in a large skillet, adding the leeks and fennel and cook for at least 10 minutes over a low flame. Add the Sambuca and stir for an additional 2 minutes. Place in a blender and puree the mixture. Return to the skillet. Add the saffron, raisins, pine nuts, and shrimp and stir frequently for an additional 5 minutes. Place over cooked pasta and serve.

Serves 4

Rolando Giuntini

Vermouth originated in Italy toward the end of the eighteenth century. It begins as a dry, white wine, and is then blended with a botanical infusion which gives it a distinctive taste. My friend Rolando, who lives in the Chianti valley of Tuscany, tells me that there are over eighty different botanical ingredients in vermouth such as flowers, fruit peels, herbs, seeds and various plants.

Italian vermouth has a bitter, spicy and caramel taste. (French vermouth has a more subtle taste, but of course I prefer the Italian.) Italians drink their vermouth straight up and also cook with it. When I asked Frank Sinatra what drink I could prepare for him, he requested a vermouth on the rocks.

SCALLOPS AND LOBSTER IN A VERMOUTH CREAM SAUCE

Flour   ¼ cup
Yellow corn meal   ¼ cup
Parsley   ¼ cup, fresh, chopped
Basil   ¼ cup, fresh, chopped
Shallots   ¼ cup, chopped fine
Red Pepper flakes   ¼ cup
Cheese, Parmesan   ¼ cup, grated
Sea Scallops   2 lbs., extra large, rinsed
Lobster meat   1 lb., cooked, claws left whole
Vermouth   ½ cup
Cream   1 cup, heavy
Butter   ¼ lb. sweet
Salt   ½ tsp. kosher

In a mixing bowl, combine the flour, cornmeal, parsley, basil, shallots, red pepper flakes, cheese and salt. Blend well. Add ¼ cup of vermouth and mix again. Dip the scallops and lobster in the mix and coat well. Meanwhile, melt the butter in a large skillet. On a low flame, sauté the scallops and lobster on both sides for 3 minutes. Remove the fish and set aside on paper towels. Add the remaining vermouth and the heavy cream and stir.

Serve the fish over a nest of well-drained salted spinach, pouring the remaining vermouth and cream from the skillet on top of the fish.

Serves 4

Soups

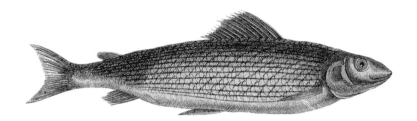

The author eating mussels in Capri.

The Procopio family originally came from San Pietro di Maida. This strong Calabrese family migrated all over the world. You can find Procopios in the Boston area, New Hampshire, California, Hawaii, Argentina, Brazil, New Zealand and all over Italy and France.

When I was a young boy, my Uncle Giovanni Procopio told me that there was a Procopio on the Mayflower. He further told me that the ship was built in Genoa. I believed him.

My uncle had ten married brothers who had a gang of children. Today, they are chefs in Florida, restaurant owners in France, hotel proprietors in New Hampshire, pear farmers in New Zealand, manufacturers of tennis rackets in Brazil, pineapple farmers in Hawaii, authors in California, salami and sausage makers in New Hampshire, a bishop in Italy, a banker in Rhode Island and an economist from New York.

This is a recipe that was given to me by the grandson of Giovanni Procopio, Chef Michael.

ZUPPA DI COZZE ALLA PROCOPIO
(Procopio's Mussel Soup)

Clean the mussels with a small flat knife or stiff brush. Remove all barnacles, sand and their "beards." Wash thoroughly in cold water a few times.

In a sauté pan, lightly brown one onion and three cloves of finely-chopped garlic in olive oil. Add a teaspoon of red crushed pepper, six leaves of fresh bay leaf and the juice from one lemon. Drop in 2 pounds of fresh-diced tomatoes. Add 1 cup of dry white wine and one cup of chicken broth and simmer for 15 minutes. Now add the 4 quarts of mussels, stirring lightly. Cook until shells are open.

This is a simple, easy and intensely flavored dish. Pour over 2 pounds of vermicelli al dente, arranging mussels on top with sprigs of fresh parsley.

Serves 6

Whenever I talk to World War II veterans who occupied the seaport city of Livorno, Italy, they immediately identify with the food and culture of this area.

Livorno was founded in the fifteenth century and is the gateway to the Tuscan region. It is close to Pisa, Viareggio, Lucca, Montecatini and an hour's drive by car to Florence.

A century later, Saphardic Jews, orthodox Greeks, Armenians, Englishmen and Frenchmen came to Livorno to escape religious persecution. It became a melting pot of different nationalities and unusual styles of cooking.

Every time I visit Italy, I spend a few days in Livorno and frequent the great restaurants. I usually complete my trip by going up to the beautiful mountain retreat of Montenero, where I make peace with myself, and pray at the *Santuario di Montenero*. Many pilgrims from Italy visit Montenero because of their faith and devotion to Mary of Montenero, the patron saint of Tuscany.

Many years ago while I was touring this magnificent and *antichiassimo* sactuary, I met a very old Armenian monk. He is a compassionate and peaceful man with a soft voice. Brother Boghos had just turned 92 years old and I remembered his *compleanno* with a small gift of ouzo. We celebrated his birthday at the Ristoranti Di Conti, known for its superb fish soup, especially their signature dish, *Cacciucco,* which comes from the Arab word cuscus. ("Cuscussua" is a mix of many different influences and the ingredients in this fish soup will vary occasionally). Brother Boghos introduced me to the proprietor, Signor Conti Antonio, whose father was Italian and whose mother Yeva was Armenian. The whole family worked in the kitchen together. The fresh *spezie* were flying and the aroma from the cooking held me *prigioniero*. I didn't want to leave so I asked Antonio if I could rent an apartment upstairs unseen. He said, *"Sfortunato, occupato con cugini."*

Brother Boghos told me that according to the history of the Armenians, his people were ruled by Greeks, Russians, Arabs and Persians, all of whom had a great influence on Armenian food and its preparation. In the following recipe, I am using an Arab vegetable called okra. The Arabs called it "bomies" and it originated on the basin of the Nile River in Egypt. Brother Boghos told me that Armenian food is considered one of the most elaborate in the world.

Although this recipe is Italian, it is influenced by the Arabs and the Greeks. Incidentally, ouzo, the gift I gave Brother Boghos, is also used in this recipe. It originated in Russia and was brought to Greece in 1860 by Efstathios Barbayannis to the island of Lesvos. He had the experience and knowledge of the distillation process of ouzo.He used a secret blend of aniseed and many rare and sweet-smelling herbs. To this day, his family continues to bottle ouzo for all of Greece and the world.

ZUPPA CON PESCE ALLA MONTENERO
(Soup with Fish from Montenero)

Onion   2 medium, chopped
Celery   6 stalks, chopped
Pepper   1 red
Fennel   1 stalk, chopped
Garlic   6 cloves, chopped
Olive Oil, extra virgin   2 Tbsp
Tomatoes   6 large, chopped or 28-oz. can plum
Broth   1 qt. vegetable
Basil   6 leaves, fresh, chopped
Parsley   1 Tbsp. fresh, chopped
Red Pepper flakes   1 Tbsp. crushed
Ouzo   ½ cup, Greek
Fish (cod, sole or halibut)   3 lbs. fillets
Okra   1 lb. fresh
Couscous   10 oz. plain

In a large skillet, sauté the onion, celery, chopped pepper, fennel and garlic in olive oil on a medium flame for 10 minutes or until tender, stirring frequently. Add the tomatoes, vegetable broth, basil, parsley, pepper flakes and ouzo. Simmer covered for 20 minutes. Add the desired fish and okra and cook on a low flame for an additional 10 minutes.

Meanwhile, in a medium saucepan, bring water, salt and 1 tsp. olive oil to a boil. Stir in the couscous and cover. Remove from flame and set aside for 5 minutes. Place couscous in small, oiled custard dishes to form little molds. Serve the fish soup in large soup dishes and gently place the formed couscous molds inverted on top with a leaf of fresh basil. Now it looks like Montenero!

Serves 6

Faro is an ancient grain that was found in Etruscan tombs and is being used today in a variety of recipes in Tuscany. It may be available at your Italian grocery market or you might buy some on your next trip to Tuscany. Being very sensitive to tastes and smells, I have recalled this recipe on my most recent visit to the town of Castelfranco di Sotto Pisa in Tuscany. On Sundays, I would join the local *aficionados* at a colorful hilltop *ristorante* called Nando's. It is known for its Tuscan specialties such as faro, lentils and leafy vegetables mixed with the fruits of the sea. They prepare pure rustic farm cooking that doesn't compromise quality and flavor.

Before the mid-day meal arrived, I would usually drink a few glasses of wine (made from Sangiovese grapes with no sulfites added) and eat a whole loaf of unsalted crusty bread made in the wood-fired oven. I would dunk the bread in a dish of pure green extra virgin olive oil before the antipasto greeted me with salami and roasted peppers accompanied by hard ricotta cheese and Tuscan herbs and spices. One time, I asked a locale *barone*, who was 96 years old why his hair was still brown. He said, "It's the olive oil in our diet." He went through two wives and the latest, Sophia, a Polish woman, is 56 years old. He always has a smile and a twinkle in his eyes and seems to be very happy. God bless him. Olive oil, *vino* and pasta may be the answer.

Italian cuisine since classical times has been intense, gratifying, alive, fresh and authentic.

The dining room at Nando's is always filled, but we like the outside patio where we dine stylishly under grapevines. Nando greets me warmly and kisses me on both cheeks. This is the custom in Italy. He points to the view of the town below: the olive trees show shadows of silver and are hung with white nets (the harvest of the olives starts in November.) There are chestnut trees that are a staple of the area for the production of chestnut flour, fields of wheat, barley and sunflowers and the fossilized grape vines that call out to Bacchus. This is the famous Chianti Classico region that has the black rooster on the neck of the wine bottle. Puffs of smoke can also be seen around the ancient hill towns. It is that time of year for burning the trimmings from the manicured grape vines and the harvesting of *funghi*. All the restaurants in the area have mushrooms on their menus, particularly

The author with nando.

the porcini mushrooms made with homemade pasta or risotto. When I return to the states, you would always find a few packages of dried porcini in my suitcase.

As I look out from the patio, I can see church towers peeking through the tall rows of cypresses. In the distance, you could see the outline of Garibaldi Park that was built by Mussolini. Many of the old timers still praise him for the train stations, bridges and parks he built. The Palazzo del Commune, the seat of local government in Castelfranco di Sotto Pisa, has a large wall fortifying the town hall which is covered with coats of arms made of majolica that belonged to the local notables of years past. In a passionate voice, Nando would say, "*Bella Italia.*" Suddenly, interrupting my *paesano*, church bells could be heard all over the valley, coming from these medieval towns. People were getting married and the horns of the small Fiats and Lancias were announcing the arrival of the bride. Music could be heard as small orchestras were tuning up for the parties soon to start under the grapevines behind the brides' homes. There were at least six towns around this area and is still today *paradiso*. I acknowledged to Nando, "*Si, bella, bella Italia.*" I knew all of these towns so well and I have a love affair with all of them, particularly the towns that have small markets that specialize in a variety of products from *formaggio* (cheese) to *carne* (meat) with rabbits and young goats hanging in their windows framed by homemade sausages. And oh, the pastry shops! My favorite treat is the sponge cake filled with almonds, hazelnuts, chocolate and cream that looks like a cardinal's skull cap. In this area can be found excellent *trattorias* and restaurants; in fact, the best in Italy.

One night, I had a wonderful meal of pork and prunes at the Ristorante Enoteca in Montopoli. It was *straordinario*! Tuscans really know how to eat, live and live long. They have a *carnivale* every day of their lives with *festas*, and *sagras* celebrating wine, food, family and *amici*. *Vivere! Vivere!* My heart is here in the hills of Tuscany where this deep love of life is always present and shared. When I return to the states, I think about Tuscany; I cry to return to the *campagna* and its natural beauty.

Twenty of my wife's cousins would join us at Nando's for this culinary feast and we *bacio* all of them. We have a lot to learn from these *pisans* and Florentines. They know what they are doing and how to do it. So did Leonardo da Vinci.

ZUPPA DI FARO CON PESCE
(Soup of Faro with Fish)

Olive oil, extra virgin   ½ cup
Pancetta or salt pork   3 Tbsp.
Onion   1 large, minced
Garlic   3 cloves, minced
Celery   1 cup, diced
Finnochio   3 leaves, chopped
Carrots   2 cups, diced
Basil   4 leaves, chopped
Parsley   5 sprigs, chopped
Wine, white   ½ cup
Tomatoes   3 lbs., fresh, crushed (or 1 qt. chicken soup)
Octopus or Calamari   2 lbs., buy cleaned, wash again
Mussels   3 lbs., brushed and cleaned
Faro (or long grain rice)   3 cups, pre-soaked, washed and cooked in boiling
water until   tender
Salt   1 tsp.
Red Pepper flakes   1 tsp.

In a 4-quart pot, heat the olive oil on a low flame and lightly brown the *pancetta*, onions, garlic, celery, *finnochio* and carrots. Add the basil, parsley, wine and tomatoes or chicken soup. Cook covered over a low flame for 20 minutes, stirring often. Prepare the baby octopus or calamari by removing the black veil/skin and wash thoroughly or request your fish market to prepare it for you. Wash again before cooking. Cut into small pieces and add to pot with 1 tsp. salt and 1 tsp. of

crushed red pepper flakes. Cook for 15 minutes or until tender. Add the mussels and clams and cook until shells open. Add the cooked faro and stir for 5 minutes. Arrange shellfish over this hearty thick soup. When ready to serve, drizzle olive oil on top.

Serves 6

Family and friends at Nandos.

Livorno is well known for its many fish restaurants as well as Italy's top chefs.

On a recent trip to this seaport town with my wife's *cugino* Mauro Pistolesi, a *pisan* from Castelfranco di Sotto Pisa, I discovered the secrets of cooking fish Livorno style. This particular recipe combines fish with vegetables, exotic herbs, spices and *verdure*.

Livorno can trace its roots to Armenians, Jews, Greeks, Englishmen, Dutch, Turks and many other nationalities. The Medicis from Florence, who bought the area from the Genoese in the fourteenth century, declared it an open zone to reside. The culinary influence of these immigrants is evident in the kitchens of Livorno.

ZUPPA DI LIVORNO
(Soup of Livorno)

Olive Oil, extra virgin   ½ cup
Calamari (squid)   1 lb., cleaned
Garlic   6 cloves, chopped
Onion, green   1 large, chopped
Celery   2 stalks, chopped
Parsley   ¼ cup, flat-leaf, chopped
Oregano   ¼ tsp.
Leeks   2, chopped
Fennel   1 stalk, chopped or 3 tbsp. of seed
Carrots   3, chopped
Tomatoes   6 large, fresh, diced
Sole   2 lbs. fillets
Wine, dry white   1 cup
Water   2 cups
Beans, cannelini   1 ½ cups, precooked
Salt and Pepper to taste

In a large pot, add the olive oil and heat on a low flame. Add the squid, garlic, onions, celery, parsley, oregano and other vegetables, except the beans. Stir-fry for 4 minutes. Now add the sole, tomatoes, wine, water and beans. Lower the flame and place a cover on the pot. Cook for an additional 10 minutes, stirring often.

Serves 6

FISH SOUP ALLA MOGLIE

Chicken Soup   2 quarts
Water   3 cups
Sea Scallops   1 lb., cleaned
Haddock or Cod   2 lb., fresh fillet, blanched
Asparagus, white   2 lb., cut into 1-inch pieces
Onion   1 large, diced
Garlic   2 cloves, diced
Saffron   2 sprigs
Potato   1 large, peeled and diced
Beans, cannelini   1 cup
Chick peas   1 cup
Carrots   3 medium, diced
Zucchinis   2 medium, diced
Tomatoes   2, fresh, diced
Celery   3 stalks, diced
Parsley   5 sprigs, chopped
Spinach   1 cup, cooked, chopped
Sherry   1 cup
Fennel   3 leaves, chopped
Salt and Red Pepper to taste

Place all the above in a large soup pot
and cook for 30-45 minutes on a
medium flame, stirring often.

Serves 8

Ludovico with the author. See page 83.

When my godfather Giovanni was a young boy of fourteen, he cooked with his uncle Cesare at a small trattoria on the fishing docks close to his home. Here is one of his tasty fish soups.

BRODO DI PESCE CON CAPPELLETTI
(Fish Soup with Little Hats)

Leeks   2 large, chopped
Garlic   3 cloves, chopped
Parsley   ½ cup, fresh, chopped
Basil   3 leaves, fresh
Cabbage   ½ head, chopped and blanched
Celery   3 stalks, chopped
Carrots   6, sliced
Tomatoes   2 lbs., ripe, cut up
Zucchini   2 medium, chopped fine
Fish stock from blanched fish   1 cup
Chicken stock   2 qt.
Haddock or Cod   3 lbs. fillets, blanched (reserve fish stock)
Fish heads (optional)
Beans, cannelini   1 cup, cooked
Wine, dry white   1 cup
Pasta   1 lb. cappelletti
Salt   1 tsp.

Saute the leeks, garlic, parsley, basil, cabbage, celery, carrots, garlic, herbs and spices until soft, about 5 minutes. Add the tomatoes, zucchini, both stocks, fish, beans and wine. Cook over low flame for 20 minutes. Add salt and pepper to taste.

Pour over cooked pasta (cappelletti). *Delizioso.*

Serves 6 to 8

At the Il Barone.

On another recent visit to Italy, my friend Tiziano introduced me to a local trattoria called "*Il Barone*" in the small town of Vinci. This *campestre* town is famous for the Leonardo Da Vinci Museum and Winery. Nearby, in the town of San Miniato, we stayed at the Villa Sonnino on a hill in the middle of a vineyard, known for its excellent wine and cuisine as well. Andrea Bocelli has dinner there quite often. I was pleasantly surprised that Tuesday night by the full house of patrons still there at 9:00 p.m. Italians dine late! I was impressed by the low prices and unusual menu (goat, rabbit, boar, game birds and great fish such as octopus, snail, and mussels, served with homemade pasta of all varieties.) Gastronomically speaking, this trattoria had it all. The recipe I am presenting next was one of the best meals I have had throughout Tuscany. I was invited by Ludovico, the owner, to go out back to the *cucina* to watch chef Bartolomeo (from Altopascio, well-known for chefs) prepare his food in earthenware pots and pans. While sipping Sangiovese, I watched him as he infused a variety of fresh herbs – sage, rosemary, thyme, parsley, marjoram and basil—into his different preparations. Chef Bartolomeo integrated slices of porcini mushrooms (that he had picked with his father from nearby mountains) into his tasty fish soup. He added Swiss chard at the end, which gave the meal an overwhelming flavor and fragrance.

I keep a list of great chefs in Tuscany and Bartolomeo is at the top. In my research, I found that Tuscan cooking goes back thousands of years to the Etruscans. I saw continuity in all the Tuscan kitchens I have had the pleasure to explore. Ludovico, the owner, comes from Livorno on the Versilia coast and buys all his fresh fish from family members. He once told me, "You must look a fish in the eyes to see if it is really fresh." *Bravo*, Bartolomeo and *grazia* Tiziano!

This area of Italy casts a magic spell on you when you travel through its green mountains, fields of sunflowers, wheat fields, manicured vineyards bursting with purple grapes and observe sheep roaming the pastures. But most memorable are the peasant trattorias with chianti and excellent cuisine. The people here are *sincero* and embrace you and take you into their arms.

My cousin Johnny Procopio, who is more partial to the southern Italians, says, "Tuscans really know how to live doing nothing. "*Dolce fare niente.*"

BRODO DI PESCE CON LE BIETE
(Fish Soup with Swiss Chard)

Chicken stock   2 qt., clear
Water   2 cups
Wine, white   1 cup, dry
Porcini mushrooms   4 medium, cleaned, sliced
Swiss chard   1 lb., stems removed, chopped, blanched
Beans (ceci)   2 cups, precooked chick peas
Parsley   2 Tbsp., flat-leaf, chopped
Leeks   2 medium, chopped fine
Garlic   6 cloves, chopped
Celery   3 stalks, chopped
Bay leaf   3 leaves, chopped
Tomatoes   4 medium fresh, chopped
Tomato paste   3 Tbsp.
Olive oil, extra virgin   3 Tbsp.
Red pepper   1 Tbsp., crushed
Codfish   2 lbs. fillets and large chunks, fresh
Shrimp   6 large, cooked and deveined
Tuscan bread   6 slices, oven-toasted
Salt to taste

In a large pot, add chicken stock, water, and wine. Cover and bring to a boil. Lower the flame to simmer and continue to add the remaining ingredients except for the fish. Cook for 10 minutes and stir. Add the codfish and cook, raising the flame to medium for an additional 15 minutes. Taste the soup and correct for salt.

Add the toasted bread to the individual dishes with 1 shrimp, olive oil and parsley on top.

Serves 6

Tiziano is a ceramic manufacturer in Montelupo, where he and his wife Filomena work in a stone farmhouse in the middle of a field surrounded by chickens, goats, and even a donkey. His ceramic vases and platters are sold all over Tuscany. One of his artists, Rolando, is recognized throughout the area and can be seen on local television stations.

Evelina, Tiziano and Lauren in Montelupo.

Pasta & Pollenta

ROSE COMEI'S PASTA FAGIOLI WITH COD FISH AND MUSSOLINI'S PARADE

As a young boy of eight, (whenever I stayed at my *nonna's* house on Garfield Street, and (after playing half ball behind moody school) I would visit my friend Tony Comei's house on Saturdays. He lived nearby on River Street (overlooking the Merrimack river in Haverhill, Massachusetts.) There was always a distinctive aroma of garlic cooking in salt pork that penetrated the walls of his mother Rose's third floor apartment. This particular Saturday as I ascended the staircase, I took a deep breadth and I knew instantly, that I was in for a treat (*banchetto*). Earlier, Tony alerted me about the upcoming lunch. I was always welcomed at the Comei's home. After all, my *nonno Donato* and *nonna, Costanza* came from the same town in Italy as his father Sam. Also, our mothers were very close friends.

When we arrived on the scene, the white porcelain kitchen table was set with large soup dishes that were trimmed with orange leaves. All the Italians on River Street had the same set. They came from the local Strand theater (where Tony's mother Rose and many other mothers would attend the weekly Sunday matinee just to receive free dishes). they didn't care if Tarzan was showing or Gene Autry, as long as they received the dishes. They couldn't understand English anyway. Also, on the table was a large piece of Provolone cheese on display like a magnificent piece of crystal (with a *marchio* in red to prove its authenticity) and a well used hand grater in red. The paint on the handle was chipped. Next to the old grater was a large canning jar filled with hot red pickled peppers that my mother sent over.

Tony's father Sam, a very statuesque gentleman (who migrated from Bisegna, Italy) which was a rugged and brutal mountain town in *abbruzzi* (wild goats roamed the mountain side). Sam gave the appearance of a *Colonnello* in the Italian army as he sat at the head of the table near an old Philco radio. Sam was a very stern, no-nonsense person. His entertainment was playing cards and bocce at the garibaldi club and listening to overseas broadcasts from Italy. Occasionally he would bet a horse with Louie the bookmaker for fifty cents. He always listened attentively to speeches of the one and only Benito Mussolini. You could hear Sam comment on the achievements of Mussolini " he brought stability and made the trains run on time", "and he removed the prostitutes from the streets," Sam said.

You could hear "Il Duce's" voice coming from many apartments up and down River street. All the Italian immigrants tuned in. For a moment, I thought Mussolini was leading a parade up River street, because the sons of Italy band led by Vinny deProfio suddenly started rehearsing across the street. Between the band, Mussolini's shouting and the cantor *Moshe Orenstein* (who performed at the *schul* on Washington street) on the second floor apartment below singing Yiddish songs, you thought there was an invasion of Haverhill. As I recall it today, I now realize how hilarious it was. I always had a laugh with Tony "fat" Comei.

The best of laughs I will never forget. While we waited for the meal, I surveyed the kitchen again and saw two pictures over the ice box, one of the Pope and the other of *Enrico Caruso*. In the kitchen window I noticed a black and white card that would signal the ice man below that ice was needed. Mario Santerelli was everyone's ice man on River Street. He also made wine in his cellar and sold it. He made more money on the sale of wine than the sale of ice. His son Mario, today is a very wealthy person who continues to make wine in his cellar and yes, he sells it.

That day, Rose made some wide Maltagliati-irregular triangle shapes to be added to the soup. I could see the pasta drying on a sheet in the bedroom off the kitchen. There was a statue of St. Anthony on the bureau looking down protecting the pasta. In fact, there was a religious statue in every room of the house. There was a large loaf of Schena's bread on the table (they would deliver the bread to your door back then) and Sam gestured to me to rip a piece off. Bottles of homemade wine (from Santerelli's cellar) and Cleary's orange soda for mixing with the wine adorned the table. One bottle of moxie stood alone ready to be mixed with milk.

The man on the moxie bottle looked like a doctor pointing his finger at me. (I can remember receiving a bottle or two of Moxie when I had my tonsils removed from my *comare , Marianna. " beve*, this is *medicina"* she said).

We all had our own clean kitchen towel draped around our necks instead of a napkin ready for action (*azione*).

Rose came in from the pantry where all the magic was being created with the first course of antipasto. The platter had Genoa salami, provolone cheese (that would bite your tongue), hot vinegar peppers, sardines, anchovies, large green stuffed olives, mushrooms, pickled green tomatoes, artichoke hearts, cucumbers, pickled pigs feet, capers, ceci beans, huge hard boiled eggs (they could have been duck eggs, now that I think of it) and thin veils of capacol and chunks of imported tuna. This majestic arrangement was sitting on a bed of romaine lettuce and chicory. Marinated eggplant and miniature Mozzarella balls surrounded the oval platter (that looked like eyeballs). Sam poured a dark green olive oil and sprinkled some aged balsamic vinegar from Modena on top of the *insalata*.

When Rose returned to the pantry with the sheet full of dried pasta, I saw her place a quarter in the gas meter (before the flame ran out on the stove). After Sam served the antipasto, he then poured a small portion of wine in our glasses. Tony and I then filled the rest of the glass with Cleary's orange soda (that was made up North Broadway.)

Then came the pasta fagioli in the largest bowl I have ever seen. She had enough pasta fagioli for the polish army. I couldn't refuse the third dish that Rose offered. Rose then came out with a large platter of boiled *bollito* chicken, fresh from Tony and Angie Pecci's farm. The fowl was served with its heart, liver, boiled egg yolks, good looking chicken feet and gizzards on the side of the platter. Boiled potatoes, carrots, cabbage and garlic kielbasa from John Zaminski's market was on another platter next to me. The garlic to me smelled like roses. I was oriented to this garlic smell because my *nonna* would place garlic on a string around my neck for some reason. Also, believe it or not eight large Matza balls (sent up from the *ebreo* family on the second floor) accompanied this celebration. I really don't remember what we were celebrating, but it was a real party *comitiva*.

So there you have it. I thought I had just arrived in heaven. A glorious lunch at Tony's home on River street. After the meal, Tony brought a bowl of pasta fagioli to the second floor neighbors (to this day the Orensteins don't know that the pasta fagioli started out with salt pork).

Oh, I forgot, after Rose served some fresh peeled black figs (that came from Badalato's market) with vanilla ice cream, we accompanied the colonel to the Garibaldi Club in his Studebaker (that couldn't go over 30 miles an hour). There we would listen to the old timers tell stories of Italy, hunting trips and their search for wild mushrooms. Those were the days! Memorabile!

PASTA FAGIOLI WITH COD FISH

Olive oil, (Extra Virgin)   ¼ cup
Salt Pork   1 Tbs., chopped
Fennel   ½ tsp.
Onion, White   1 large, finely chopped
Garlic   4 cloves, minced
Celery   2 sticks, finely chopped
Parsley   6 stalks, fresh
Sweet Basil   6 leaves, whole
Tomatoes, crushed   1 can, 28 ounces
Cannellini beans   3 cups, pre soaked
Carrot, large   1 finely chopped
Chicken soup   1 quart
Cod Fish   2 lbs. chopped
Pasta, Ditalini or elbow   1 lb.
Red pepper flakes   1 tsp.
Marsala or dry sherry   ¼ cup
Salt & Black pepper to taste

In a large pot on a low flame saute the onion, celery, carrot and salt pork, in olive oil (reserve some oil for the topping). After 4 or 5 minutes add the garlic and cook until lightly brown. Stir frequently. Add the tomatoes and cook for 15 minutes on a continued low flame. Stir often. Add the chicken soup. (After you have soaked the beans over night and boiled for at least 15 minutes on a low flame, rinse and drain.) Now add to the pot half of the whole beans and the remaining mashed. Incorporate the Marsala and red pepper. Add the codfish. Cook for an additional 10 minutes on a low flame. Meanwhile, cook the pasta al dente with ½ tsp. of salt and drain. (Retain a cup of broth and add to the pot.) Add the pasta to the pot (mix) and taste for salt and pepper. Sprinkle a little olive oil on top with grated Pecorino cheese. Thanks Rose. Thanks Fat. Thanks Sabatino.

Serves 6.

RIGATONI DI ASPARAGI CON ARAGOSTA E BACCALA
(Cheese with Pasta, Asparagus, Lobster and Cod)

During the *quaresima* (lent) season, meals are usually prepared with a variety of fish. In small towns in Italy, similar to Castelfranco di Sotto Pisa, the custom was to invite the local pastor for dinner. During this holy season, my wife's cousin Antonella invited us one day for this memorable dinner with Father Alessandro. He was from Palermo, the fishing center of Sicily in the fifteenth century.

MISTURA

Asparagus,   2 lbs., fresh, trimmed, cleaned, blanched
Lobster, Fresh   2 lbs. meat, cooked, chopped
Cod fish   2 lbs. cooked chopped
Rigatoni (any pasta)   1 lb. cooked
Bread Crumbs, Italian   ½ cup
Olive Oil   2 Tbsp.
Butter   ¼ cup – 1 stick
Olive Oil   2 Tbsp.
Carrots   2, medium, chopped fine
Shallots   1 medium, chopped fine
Onion   1 medium, chopped fine
Garlic   3 cloves, minced
Celery   2 stalks, chopped fine
Heavy cream   1 cup

Cheese, Parmesan   ½ cup, grated
Mozzarella   ½ cup, chopped
Eggs   2, beaten
Lemon   1 juice from
Marsala wine   ¼ cup
Parsley, fresh   1 Tbsp., chopped
Salt and Pepper to taste

Boil the rigatoni until al dente and set aside. Sprinkle lightly with olive oil and mix to prevent the pasta from sticking. Coat the asparagus, lobster and cod with the bread crumbs. Rub a medium sized baking dish with olive oil and place the first layer of asparagus, lobster, cod and pasta in it. Pour equal amounts of the sauce (recipe below) on top. Continue making additional layers of asparagus/fish with sauce in between.

SAUCE PREPARATION

In a large saucepan on a low flame, melt the butter and the olive oil and sauté the carrots, shallots, onion, garlic and celery for 2 or 3 minutes. Add the cream, 1 tbsp. of flour, Parmesan, mozzarella and mix well. Remove from the flame and cool for 2 minutes. Add the eggs slowly to prevent them from cooking, and whip vigorously, adding the lemon juice, Marsala wine, salt and pepper to taste. Place back on the heat and continue whipping until you have a nice creamy sauce. Pour over the layers of asparagus, fish and pasta, reserving some sauce for topping when taking the preparation to the plate. Continue this process, making layers of asparagus, fish, pasta and cheese sauce.

Bake in a pre-heated 375° oven for 15 minutes.

Cut into 5-inch squares and pour reserved sauce on top. Sprinkle with parsley and more Parmesan cheese.

Serves 6

Although polenta originated in Venice, it has become popular all over Italy. It can be prepared with meat, fish, cabbage or mushrooms and also eaten plain with butter. Many restaurants in the states are offering it on their menus with a red sauce.

I think of polenta as a peasant dish because it is inexpensive and easy to prepare. I have eaten polenta in many of the hill towns of Italy and must tell you that my favorite presentation is with sausages, mushrooms and a red sauce; however, this recipe uses fish. Cheese with fish is not an acceptable combination for the Italians, but I have added the pecorino because it is delicious and full-flavored.

POLENTA CON COVOLO E PESCE
(Polenta with Cabbage and Fish)

Water   6 cups
Salt   1 tsp
Cornmeal, yellow   3 cups
Cabbage, white   ½ head, chopped, pre-cooked
Butter   ½ lb., melted (reserve some to sauté pancetta and onion)
Pancetta/bacon   ¼ cup, cooked, chopped
Onion   1 large, chopped, sautéed in butter
Fish   1 lb. cod fillets, boiled for 3 minutes
Cheese, pecorino   ½ cup, grated
Parsley   ¼ cup, chopped with pancetta
Tomato sauce   3 cups, Italian, prepared
Pepper to taste

In a large pot, add the water and salt. Bring to a medium boil and add the cornmeal. Lower the flame and stir quickly with a long handled wooden spoon for at least 30 minutes, making sure the cornmeal does not stick and become lumpy. A copper pan is usually used for this because copper heats evenly. Add the boiled cabbage, melted butter, fried pancetta and onions. Fold in the fish, cheese, and parsley. Whip the mixture well for an additional 5 minutes over a low flame. Place the cooked polenta in a buttered casserole or fish mold. Pour heated tomato sauce on top and add more grated cheese. Salt and pepper to taste.

Serves 6

Orecchiete are small, ear-shaped pasta. I was told by a local *bugiardo* (liar) in San Miniato, that they were shaped to mimic the local priests' ears and prepared on Fridays.

92

The unique flavor of this recipe has a rustic character. It uses white cannellini beans that are famous in Tuscany. Tuscans, known as *"mangiafagioli"* or "bean eaters", eat some type of beans every day and wash them down with the wonderful wine of the Chianti Valley.

ORECCHIETTE DI PADRE CON CAVOLO E GAMBERO
(Pasta Ears with Cabbage and Shrimp)

Onion   1 large, chopped
Garlic   2 cloves, chopped
Olive oil, extra virgin   ½ cup
Butter   ¼ stick
Basil   4 leaves, chopped
Parsley (cilantro)   4 sprigs, chopped
Tomatoes   3 large, ripe, chopped
Cabbage (or cauliflower)   1 head, precooked, chopped
Salt to taste
Red Pepper   1 tsp., crushed
Chicken broth   1 qt.
Shrimp   1 lb. medium size, cleaned, pre-cooked
Cannelini beans   1 ½ cups, precooked
Pasta   1 lb. orrecchiette (look for it in your local Italian market)
White truffle oil   1 tsp.

Lightly brown the onion and garlic in olive oil and butter. Add the basil, parsley, tomatoes, cabbage, salt and pepper. Saute for 5 minutes. Place in a 4-qt. Pot and add the chicken broth. Cook covered on low heat for 30 minutes, stirring often. Add the shrimp and beans and cook for an additional 10 minutes on low heat. Boil the orrecchiette in a separate pot of salted water (1 tsp.) until al dente. Drain and place in pot with cabbage and broth. Stir in the truffle oil.

Serves 6

All summer long, day after day, San Pietro di Maida has a festival celebrating saints and food. There are more saint days and holy days and celebrations of food here than in any other country in the world. One town will celebrate cooked *coniglio* (rabbit), another gnocchi and wine. Others will set aside special days to bless the fishermen. And don't forget the harvest with its purple eggplant that is grown in abundance in southern Italy. It can be fried, made in a sauce, rolled and stuffed with cheese or roasted in sauce, rubbed with olive oil and grilled.

This is a great way to eliminate meat on Fridays and incorporate shellfish with eggplant and cheese.

Prepare a salad to accompany this hearty meal.

LASAGNA CON MELANZANE, GAMBERETTI E ARAGOSTA
(Lasagna with Eggplant, Shrimp and Lobster)

Eggs   3, beaten
Milk   ½ cup
Oregano   ½ tsp.
Nutmeg   ½ tsp.
Basil   6 leaves, chopped
Bread Crumbs, Italian   2 cups
Eggplant   4 large, sliced
Garlic   2 cloves, whole
Olive Oil   1 cup
Tomato Sauce   1 qt. precooked
Lasagna   1 lb. cooked in salt water
Ricotta Cheese   1 lb., mixed with 1 egg, salt
Pecorino Cheese   1 cup, grated
Shrimp   1 lb. precooked, whole
Lobster Meat   1 lb. precooked, pieces
Mozzarella Cheese   1 lb., sliced
Butter   2 Tbsp.
Salt and Pepper to taste

In a medium sized bowl, blend the eggs with ½ cup of milk. Add salt, pepper, oregano, nutmeg and basil. Spread the Italian bread crumbs on a flat dish. Slice the eggplant in ½ inch pieces (half dollar shape) and dip them in the bowl of eggs and milk. Remove and coat both sides with bread crumbs. Lightly brown the garlic in the olive oil and remove from skillet. Place eggplant slices into skillet with warm olive oil on a medium flame and brown on both sides, then set aside.

In a buttered rectangular pan covered with tomato sauce, place the first layer of cooked lasagna, then a layer of eggplant. Spread the mixed ricotta on top, add the shrimp, lobster meat and mozzarella cheese. Sprinkle grated pecorino cheese on top and spread the prepared tomato sauce, reserving some for serving later. Continue with the same procedure, layering again. Bake in preheated 375° oven with a tinfoil cover for 15 minutes. Serve with reserved sauce and grated cheese.

Serves 6 to 8

Vegetables

POMODORO SORPRESA
(Stuffed Tomatoes Surprise)

Eggplant   1 small, peeled and diced
Lobster meat   2 cups cooked
Parsley   2 Tbsp., chopped
Basil   6 leaves, chopped
Onion   1 medium, chopped
Garlic   3 cloves, minced
Olive Oil, extra virgin   ½ cup
Bread   2 slices toasted, Italian, chopped
Vermouth (sweet)   ¼ cup
Cheese   ½ cup Parmesan, grated
Tomatoes   6 large, firm, pulp removed
Salt and Pepper

Saute the eggplant, parsley, basil, onion and garlic in olive oil. Salt and pepper to taste. Add the toasted bread, vermouth, cheese and lobster and mix well. Stuff the tomatoes and sprinkle cheese on top. Place under broiler for 3 minutes. Serve on lettuce with a sprig of basil on top.

Serves 6

One winter I visited St. Pietro a Maida in Calabria. My cousin Concetta invited me to her house for stuffed escarole. (The leaves are quite tender this time of year.) Concetta lived outside the town in an old stucco house in sun-bleached colors of beige, red and yellow. When I arrived, her husband Savario sat like a commander on the front porch, drinking wine and scratching lottery tickets that were sent from America. He was dressed as if he were going to a wedding with a black silk suit, and a red scarf around his short neck with a matching hankerchief in his jacket pocket. He was a tailor by trade and was an impeccable dresser. Concetta starched his shirts every day even though he was retired. He would strut through town with his hands folded behind his back like an *ufficiale* sent by the prime minister of Italy. He was a proud *orgoglioso* gentleman of eighty-eight but stubborn in his ways. There is an expression for this type of southern Italian: Hard Head.

This meal was so good that I overindulged by eating eight stuffed escarole!

SCAROLA RIPRENE
(Stuffed Escarole)

Escarole   1 head, cleaned, stalks removed
Potatoes   6 peeled, boiled, mashed
Bread Crumbs, Italian   1 cup
Eggs   2 large, beaten
Lobster or Crab Meat   2 cups, cooked and chopped
Parsley   2 Tbsp., chopped
Garlic   4 cloves, chopped
Onion, White   1 large, chopped
Fennel   2 Tbsp., seeds
Cheese   ½ cup Parmesan
Butter   ½ cup, melted
Vermouth   ½ cup, sweet
Lemon   1, juice from
Italian Sauce   3 cups, prepared
Salt and Red Pepper Flakes to taste

Prepare the escarole leaves ahead by blanching for at least one minute. Drain and wipe well and set aside on paper towels.

In a large mixing bowl, add all the above ingredients except the tomato sauce. Mix well.

Spread open the escarole leaves, place the stuffing on top and roll up the leaves. Place in a buttered covered baking dish and pour prepared sauce on top. Sprinkle with grated cheese and set in a preheated 375° oven for 15 minutes.

Serves 4 to 6

Southern Italy is well known for vegetables with a Greek influence. The popular eggplant is eaten all year long in a variety of ways. My *compare* would preserve them sliced in an olive oil marinade for later use when the eggplant was out of season.

The following recipe incorporates the sea and the garden to create a marvelous blend of savory flavors.

MELANZANE IMBOTTITI
(Stuffed Eggplant)

Eggplant   3, medium
Tuna   1 large can, white, drained, broken up
Eggs   3 hard-boiled, chopped; 1 beaten
Mushrooms   ½ cup, cooked, chopped
Bread crumbs, Italian   1 cup
Cheese, mozzarella or fontina   4 slices, chopped; 6 slices for eggplant topping
Basil   4 leaves, chopped
Parsley (Cilantro)   3 sprigs, chopped
Rice, white   ½ cup, precooked
Olives   1 cup, black, chopped
Tomato sauce   1 qt., prepared
Salt and Pepper to taste

Stuffed Eggplant

Cut the washed eggplant lengthwise. Hollow out the center and cut into small pieces. Fry in olive oil. Meanwhile, blanch the eggplant shells in boiling water for no more than 1 minute and drain. In a large bowl, combine the fried pieces of eggplant with the tuna. Add the chopped eggs, mushrooms, beaten egg, bread crumbs, cheese, basil, parsley, rice, salt, pepper and olives. Mix all ingredients well.

Stuff the eggplants and place in a greased baking dish. Pour tomato sauce on top and cover with tin foil. Bake in a preheated 375° oven for 30 minutes, or until eggplant shell is tender. Toward the end of cooking time, place slices of mozzarella or fontina cheese on top of eggplant and return to oven. This is wonderful with a dish of pasta, tomato sauce and a dry red wine.

Serves 6

Zucchini flowers

I look forward to market day, *mercato*, and buying unusual vegetables, fish, meat and cheese for my kitchen in Tuscany. The provisions are brought into town every Monday by large trucks that open their sides and display their fresh produce. I usually take a few large empty shopping bags with me and if the dandelions are out, I will buy a few bunches. I also look for mushrooms, zucchini flowers, anise, fresh anchovies, squid or octopus, eels, goat heads, jack rabbits, black birds and fresh sausage made with wild boar.

"Don't forget the figs", my wife Arlene will call out to me from the second floor window as I set out for the Piazza di Garibaldi. This is a small friendly town called Castelfranco di Sotto Pisa. It is a second home to me and we are very appreciative of the apartment that my wife's cousins provide us. It gives her the opportunity to wash our clothes by hand and hang them out the second floor window across a busy Strada di Fiori.

FIORI DI ZUCCA CON ACCIUGHE
(Zucchini Flowers with Anchovies)

Bread, Italian   toasted, cubed
Cornmeal   ½ cup
Parsley   ¼ cup, chopped
Cheese, parmesan   ¼ cup, grated
Egg   1 large
Olive oil, extra virgin   ¼ cup
Salt and Pepper
Fiori di Zucca (zucchini flowers)   12 , closed for freshness
Anchovies   12 fillets
Dandelions   1 large bunch
Bread crumbs, Italian   ½ cup
Flour   ½ cup
Basil   12 whole
Lemon   1, juice from

In a medium mixing bowl, add all the ingredients except the flowers, anchovies, dandelions, basil, lemon juice, bread crumbs and flour. Mix well. Prepare the zucchini flowers by making a slit on the side and removing the pistils. Stuff the flowers with the mix, handling the flowers gently. Also place one anchovy and one bay leaf inside each one.

On a large plate, mix the flavored bread crumbs, corn meal and flour. Place the flowers in this mix and coat well. Heat the olive oil over a medium flame and fry the flowers until they are lightly browned. Remove them with a slotted spatula and place on paper towels to absorb excess oil.

Spread the cleaned and dry dandelions on a large platter with the zucchini flowers on top and sprinkle with lemon juice and olive oil. Add salt and pepper to taste.

Serves 2

The author in Impruneta.

Autumn is a wonderful time to visit Tuscany, with its crisp days and cool nights. This is the hunting season for wild boar and game birds, the time when the vineyards come alive and the search for white truffles and the famous porcini mushrooms begins.

The area of San Miniato is well known for all of these culinary pleasures, particularly the truffles and porcini mushrooms. Dogs with keen senses of smell are trained to locate truffles for their owners. Porcini mushrooms are picked by experienced locals for sale to restaurants as well as for their own consumption. These *cacciatores* will reveal the secret location of these exotic duos only to their immediate families.

In the fall, every restaurant in Tuscany serves both these delectables with a variety of pastas and sauces. At the Villa Sonnino, they prepare the porcini mushrooms with pappardelle pasta in a rich cream sauce with shaved truffles on top. The truffle has a very distinct scent and taste which blends very nicely with the porcini mushrooms.

TARTUFI CON PORCINI E PAPPARDELLE
(Truffles with Porcini Mushrooms and Wide Noodles)

Truffle   1 oz. fresh, shaved
Porcini mushrooms   2 cups, dry, pre-sliced into strips
Butter   ½ cup
Cream, heavy   1 cup
Thyme   ½ tsp.
Cheese, Parmesan   ½ cup, grated; ½ cup shaved
Vermouth, sweet   ¼ cup
Corn starch   1 Tbsp.
Pappardelle   1 lb.

Basil   6 leaves fresh
Salt and Pepper to taste

Clean the truffle with a light brush. The porcini mushrooms should soak for 4 or 5 hours and then drained well for at least 1 hour. Over a low flame, melt the butter in a skillet with high sides. Add the cream, thyme and Parmesan cheese. Blend with a whisk and add the vermouth and mushrooms, continuing to stir. Slowly add the corn starch, using whisk, and cook for 10 minutes over a very low flame. Add salt and pepper to taste.

In a large pot, boil the pasta in salted water until al dente. Drain well and place in the skillet with the mushroom sauce. Mix the pasta well and place in a large oval plate. Add the shaved truffle and Parmesan cheese on top and garnish with basil leaves.

Serves 4

When I visited my grandfather Donato's *paese* in Bisegna, Italy, I was invited for dinner at the home of distant relatives. I got the following recipe from *cugino* Taberio. His home sits on a cliff high in the hills of the national forest. In the distance I could see wild goats roaming the mountainside. My grandfather was born in this house in the 1800's. My grandmother Constanza was born across the street. She came from the Degiacomo family, which had 23 children. There are 60 struggling inhabitants remaining in this *rustico* town. All of the younger people have left the area for work in the large cities of Italy and Europe. Many migrated to Haverill, Massachusetts.

I happened to be in this remote village on a Friday to observe an open truck struggling up the mountainside, his horn blaring to announce his arrival in the town. Weather permitting, the peddler would make weekly trips to sell his fruit, vegetables, cured salami, sausages, cheese and meat. Because there were no stores or markets in town, the old timers would rely on this mobile market to survive. Some of the people would place special orders for certain items. If they didn't have gardens, goats for milk and cheese, they would wait for the vendor. The terrain is rugged in these mountains and the weather is brutal in the winter. But broccoletti and garlic grow wild there and are picked into the late fall.

During the war, the locals survived on chestnuts, which they ground into flour for bread. The stone ovens in the homes are still used for baking bread and there is always a copper pot hanging near the fire for polenta., which was often prepared with wild mushrooms and homemade sausages.

BROCCOLETTI CON UVETTA E PINOLI
(Broccoli Rabe with Raisins and Pine Nuts)

Broccoli Rabe   2 lbs., stems removed
Pasta, linguini   2 lbs.
Garlic   6 cloves, chopped
Onion   1 medium, chopped
Olive oil, extra virgin   ¼ cup
Bay leaves   6 fresh, chopped
Parsley   ¼ cup fresh, chopped
Pinola nuts   ½ cup, whole
Raisins   ½ cup
Lemon   1, juice from
Cheese, pecorino   ¼ cup, grated
Salt and Red Pepper to taste

Boil the pasta (al dente – 10 minutes or less) and broccolini in separate pots of salted water. Meanwhile, heat the olive oil and add garlic, onions, herbs and spices and cook in a large skillet until lightly browned. Stir in the lemon juice, raisins, pinoli nuts and salt and pepper. Once the broccolini and pasta are cooked and drained, add both to the skillet, gently stirring. Cook for 5 minutes. Place in a large bowl, arranging the broccolini on top. Sprinkle with cheese.

Serves 4

My godfather Giovanni always prepared brussels sprouts in combination with ripe tomatoes from his garden up on the "Torre di Jack."

"Always soak these *cavolo* in lemon juice," he told me. "Peel the yellow outer leaves and trim the stems before soaking." He went on to say, "The Romans gave the seeds to the Belgians and they cultivated them around the 1200's. They should be called Italian sprouts."

"Leave it to the Italians," he said, proudly looking like an *autorita* with a large audience made up of his cronies, all with large, red noses, half in the bag. "If it wasn't for the Italians," he continued , "we would all have starved." Now his audience, leaning on his garden fence, urged him on. "Giovanni, *parla, parla*." Someone in the audience shouted, "*Cante, cante*, Giovanni" but Giovanni was already singing. *Compare* Giovanni, who had been drinking wine most of the day, became a musical *oratore con autorita* (orator with audience). His voice became operatic and he would sing "if it wasn't for Columbus, Europe wouldn't have corn for polenta, potatoes for gnocchi or chocolate for gelato." *Compare* Giovanni continued for at least an hour and ended his musical speeches by inviting everyone to his kitchen for pasta e cavoli al salsa, and more vino and singing.

This is a very nourishing meal, particularly with the combination of Brussels sprouts and tomatoes.

PASTA E CAVOLINI AL SALSA
(Pasta and Brussels Sprouts in Sauce)

Salt pork/pancetta   2 Tbsp., chopped
Olive oil, extra virgin   ¼ cup
Onions   3 medium, chopped
Peppers   2 each red, green, yellow, sliced
Celery   2 stalks, chopped
Carrots   6 sliced
Mushrooms, white button   2 cups, sliced
Garlic   8 cloves, chopped
Tomatoes   5 lbs. ripe, sliced
Tomato Paste   1 12-oz. Can
Parsley   6 sprigs, chopped
Wine, dry white   1 cup
Bay leaves   12 leaves fresh, chopped
Brussels Sprouts   5 lbs., cleaned
Lemons   2, juice from
Red Pepper flakes   ¼ cup
Cheese, pecorino   1 cup, grated
Pasta, orecchiette   3 lbs. "little ears"

In a large skillet, cook the salt pork in the olive oil over a low flame. Add the onion, peppers, celery, carrots, mushrooms and sauté, stirring, for 10 minutes. Then add garlic to the skillet and cook until lightly browned. Add the diced tomatoes, paste, parsley and mix well. Pour the wine into the sauce, add the bay leaves, uncooked Brussels sprouts, lemon juice and the red pepper flakes. Stir well. Cook covered, for at least 20 minutes, stirring often. Add salt to taste.

Boil 3 lbs. of orecchiette in a large pot of salted water until al dente. Place the drained pasta in a large bowl and mix well with the sauce. Sprinkle with pecorino cheese.

Serves 6

The author as a movie producer.

The author with new found friends in Sicili, Sicily.

THE COLORS OF ITALY

The following recipe was influenced by my visit to Sicili, an ancient town in Sicily in the province of Ragusa. I was accompanied by my friend Rosetta, *mia moglia* and three elderly authorities on vegetables – women who packed vegetables for 70 years. It was a Monday morning, the day area farmers brought their produce to town. The three women were dressed in black as they had been for many years since their husbands passed away. Each of their faces was distinguished by a gold tooth in front, a large mole, and what appeared to be a slight mustache. Each had white hair pulled back tightly into a bun. These women knew everyone in town and stopped to have brief conversations with them. The men were indeed gentlemen, tipping their hats and offering kind words to the ladies who embraced them with a kiss on both cheek, and a pinch.

I was told that the economy was always good in this region because of the farming and fishing industries. Many of the packing houses prepared vegetables and fish for all of Europe. One of the women, Rosetta's mother Teresa, was a bit of a joker. She introduced me as a director of films from Hollywood, and asked her friends to pose for pictures. I took advantage of the introduction and quickly took digital pictures. One old-timer asked, "Will I receive a royalty if the movie is a success?" I responded by asking for his name and address. For a moment, the other two women thought that Teresa's comment was true and also offered their addresses. Word spread throughout the *piazza* that a Hollywood producer was in town searching for the ideal site for a movie. This created a *frenesia* of poses from everyone in the square. Women on third floor apartments posed on balconies and young women in the square produced enormous smiles. It was hilarious when word then spread that Sophia Loren might possibly be in the film. One *scherzo* by Teresa and the story expanded so swiftly that for a moment, I actually did feel like a movie producer! Did I take advantage of the moment? You bet I did. I was offered more figs, shots of *Strega*, and pizza with anchovies and hot peppers than you could imagine. And yes, I developed *stomaco acido*, or *agita*.

Finally, we arrived at the outdoor market and were suddenly in a field of vegetables of so many beautiful colors. Green and yellow zucchini, red, green and orange peppers, purple and white eggplants, green and white spears of asparagus, huge red and yellow tomatoes, white and brown mushrooms of many different varieties, red, purple and white onions the size of grapefruit, yellow corn, different types of potatoes that were black, white and brown, stalks of green celery and fennel, green parsley and cilantro, thyme, rosemary, bay leaf, dried oregano, huge strings of white garlic, enormous leaves of green and white Romaine lettuce, fava beans, green and yellow string beans, white cannellini beans, fresh green peas, and so on. Wow! The colors of Italy were out there in the Piazza of Sicili, Sicily. Here I was with Teresa, Rosetta, *mia moglia*, and Sophia Loren!

Italians are passionate about vegetables. They create wonderful salads, soups and main entrees with them. In this recipe, I have incorporated anchovies to give the presentation an added zing.

LEGUMI GRIGLIA CON ACCIUGHE
(Grilled Vegetables with anchovies)

Olive oil, extra virgin   ½ cup
Wine, red   ¼ cup
Butter   1 stick, melted
Anchovies   2, minced
Garlic   2 cloves, minced
Shallots   3 Tbsp., minced
Parsley   ½ cup fresh, chopped
Basil   6 leaves fresh, chopped
Thyme   1 tsp. dried
Lemon juice   2 Tbsp.

Puree the above ingredients in a blender until smooth. Brush on the vegetables below (both sides) and arrange in a grilling basket and grill on a hot barbecue.

Zucchini, green and yellow   3, sliced lengthwise
Peppers, red, green, yellow   slice in quarters
Tomatoes   6, ½ inch slices
Fennel   6 stalks, sliced lengthwise
Onions, white   2, ½ in inch slices
Asparagus   10 spears
Mushrooms, extra large   10, stems removed
Eggplant, purple or white   2, sliced lengthwise
Garlic   3 whole bulbs
Salt and Pepper to taste
Pizza, thick Sicilian   2, well done

After grilling vegetables, remove with tongs and arrange on Sicilian pizza. Sprinkle with shavings of Parmesan cheese and extra virgin olive oil. This is nice with a fresh Romaine salad.

Serves 6

Eggplants are plentiful in southern Italy and are prepared in many different ways as presented in this cookbook. My friends Sam and Mary Jean shared this recipe with me on my recent visit to their restaurant "Bella Vista" in an ancient town called Agrigento.

When you go shopping for eggplant, look for shiny, long eggplants that are very dark purple. This type usually doesn't have too many seeds.

MELANZANE ALLA ARAGOSTA
(Eggplant with Lobster)

Eggplant   16 slices, ½" thick
Olive oil, extra virgin   2 Tbsp.
Tomatoes   10 medium, stewed
Garlic   ¼ cup, chopped
Fennel   ¼ cup seeds
Tomato paste   3 Tbsp.
Marsala wine   ¼ cup
Lemon   2, juice from
Lobster meat   1 lb., precooked, chopped
Butter   ¼ lb.
Cream   1 cup
Cheese, Parmesan   ½ cup, grated
Mozzarella   ½ cup, grated
Ricotta Cheese   ½ cup
Eggs   2, hard boiled, chopped
Egg yolks   2, whipped
Flour   2 Tbsp.
Bread crumbs
Scallions   3, chopped

Before cooking, salt the slices of eggplant on both sides and place in a colander to drain for at least 40 minutes. Wipe any excess water off the eggplants. Bake the *melanzane* circles on a sheet pan coated with olive oil in a preheated 350° oven. Set aside. Meanwhile, sauté the tomatoes, garlic and fennel with the tomato paste over a low flame for 15 minutes. Add the Marsala, lemon juice and lobster meat and cook and stir for an additional 10 minutes. Salt and pepper to taste. Set aside off the flame.

In a skillet with high sides, melt the butter and add the cream which has been blended with the egg yolks and flour, Parmesan, mozzarella, ricotta and hard boiled eggs. Whisk the cream and cheese well and cook over a very low flame for 5 minutes or until it thickens. Set aside. Prepare the shrimp and scallops in bread crumbs and place in a skillet with butter and scallions until lightly browned on both sides

Spoon the tomato sauce and lobster onto the eggplant and return to a preheated 375° oven for 10 minutes. Remove with spatula and place on top of pasta with dollops of the warm cream sauce on top. Set the large shrimp on top with the seared scallops. Sprinkle more Parmesan cheese on top with fresh leaves of basil standing up like trees.

Serves 6

Garlic strings in the market place.

Sam and Mary Jean Argiento.

Vegetables are plentiful in Sicily and are used all year long. Cauliflower is one of the many vegetables that can be used with this recipe and it makes a hearty meal with any kind of fish. I have used beet greens, peppers, spinach, zucchini, peas, fennel, radicchio, mushrooms, carrots and many other vegetables. The Italians are known to cook extra vegetables and save some leftovers for a wonderful frittata to be made the next day.

FRITTATA ALLA VERDURA CON PESCE E PASTA
(Frittata with Vegetables and Fish)

Eggs   1 dozen fresh, blended
Cream   ½ cup
Cheese, ricotta   ½ cup
Olive oil, extra virgin   ½ cup
Onion   1 large, chopped
Garlic   4 cloves, chopped
Potato   2 medium, cooked, sliced
Cauliflower   1 head, pre-cooked and separated
Fennel   1 Tbsp. Seeds
Vegetables   leftovers (spinach, mushrooms, etc.), chopped
Cheese, mozzarella   ½ cup, chopped
Tomato   1 large, diced
Pasta   ¼ lb. angel hair, cooked and drained
Fennel   6 leaves for garnish
Fish   1 lb. cooked and flaked (whatever is available or left over from a previous meal)
Salt and Pepper to taste

In a large bowl, blend the eggs, cream and ricotta cheese and set aside. In a very large skillet, lightly brown the onion, garlic, potato and vegetables over a low flame. Work in the anchovies, fennel seeds and tomato while cooking. Add salt and pepper to taste. Once the vegetables are brown, add the egg mixture and cooked pasta and blend together. Continue cooking over a low flame, lifting the edges of the frittata to allow the eggs to circulate in the pan. Sprinkle the mozzarella cheese on top and place the skillet under the broiler. Allow the frittata and cheese to brown. Place on a large plate and garnish with twigs of fennel leaves.

Serves 6

Sauces

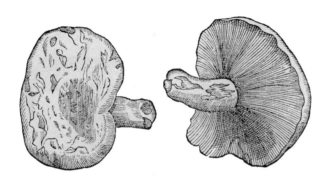

COGNAC CREAM SAUCE

Butter   ½ lb.
Heavy Cream   1 pint
Flour   ½ cup
Eggs   2 egg yolks
Cheese   ½ cup, grated, Italian
Cognac   ½ cup, reserve some for basting fish
Salt and Pepper to taste

Add slowly to the melted butter, pre-heated heavy cream, flour, portion of cognac, salt and pepper, stirring constantly. This should take 5 to 10 minutes on a low flame. Remove from flame and briskly beat in the egg yolks and cheese.

LOBSTER CREAM SAUCE

Butter   ¼ lb.
Garlic   1 clove, minced
Shallots   2, medium, finely chopped
Celery   1 stalk, finely chopped
Carrot   1, finely chopped
Spinach   1 cup cooked, drained
Flour   3 Tbsp.
Marsala wine   1 cup
Cream, heavy   ¾ cup
Salt and Pepper   1 tsp. each
Lobster   ½ lb., cooked and flaked

On a low flame, melt the butter in a sauté pan and add the garlic, shallots, celery, carrot, and lightly brown, stirring often. Add the flour and cook for 15 seconds, again stirring constantly. Add the wine and bring to a slight boil. Add the cream, spinach, cooked chopped lobster, salt and pepper. Turn heat to simmer and stir constantly with a whisk for 5 minutes until you have a smooth sauce. Pour over dish. Place pieces of lobster on top.

SALSA SUBITO
(Quick Tomato Sauce)

Olive oil, extra virgin   2 Tbsp.
Garlic   3 cloves, chopped
Onion   1 small white, chopped
Salt pork/pancetta   1 tsp., chopped fine
Tomatoes   6 ripe, chopped
Tomato paste   2 Tbsp.
Lemon   1 large, juice from
Basil   6 sprigs fresh, chopped
Vermouth, sweet   ½ cup
Anchovies   2 fillets, chopped
Capers   ½ cup, rinsed
Olives, black   ½ cup, chopped
Salt to taste
Red Pepper flakes   1 Tbsp.
Pasta, angel hair   1 lb.
Cheese, Parmesan   ½ cup, grated

In a large skillet, sauté the garlic and onion in olive oil with salt pork until very lightly browned. Add the chopped tomatoes, tomato paste, lemon and basil and cook, covered, for 15 minutes over a low flame stirring often. Remove the cover and add the vermouth, anchovies, capers, olives, salt and red pepper to taste. Stir every few minutes and cook for an additional 10 minutes over a low flame with-

out the cover. (Sometimes I will add cooked shrimp during the last 5 minutes of cooking.)

Meanwhile, boil the angel hair pasta in a large pot of water with one tsp. salt. Cook until al dente. Plate the pasta and pour the sauce on top. Sprinkle with grated Parmesan cheese.

This meal goes well with a cucumber and fresh fennel salad mixed with olive oil, balsamic vinegar, lemon juice, and a sprinkle of oregano on top.

Serves 4

116

Favorite Locations in Tuscany for a Picnic

Vinci

Every time I visit the birthplace of Leonardo da Vinci, I feel that at one time in the past I have met him. I have repeatedly visited his home in Anchiano, where we often picnic and talk to the tenant farmers who are working the terraced land. It is here in this hill country in central Tuscany, close to San Miniato, Florence, Lucca, Pisa and Siena. Anchiano is an agricultural area producing primarily wine and olive oil. I have hiked various trails through the hills of Montalbano and have had wonderful picnics here. We have also had some impromptu picnics within sight of the Guidi Castle that now houses the Museo Leonardiano. Inside that museum is one of the largest and most original collections of machines and models of the inventor, Leonardo. A wealth of interesting artistic and historical material can be viewed in the cellars of the castle as well.

The Leonardo celebrations are held during April and May. I would suggest a visit during this period to get involved in the "Lettura Vinciana," a day of Leonardo studies.

Also, be sure to visit the Cantina (Leonardo Winery) and sample the varieties of wine for your picnic. There are a few deli-type markets in the square of Vinci where I have purchased crusty Tuscan bread, provolone, sardines, prosciutto, olives, tomatoes and roasted peppers. Sprinkle the bread with the rich green virgin olive oil that this area is famous for and make a nice sandwich.

A Picnic Overlooking Il Tempo di San Biago in Montepulciano

Usually, when I leave the spa town of Chianciano Terme, I take the back road to Montepulciano, a town famous for its *vino nobile*. On the way, I will stop to pick up food and wine for our picnic. On the twenty-five minute drive to Pienza, we stop for out picnic in the pastoral area next to the temple of San Bagio in a quiet Tuscan country setting outside the walls of Montepulciano. It is considered to be one of the most significant churches of the renaissance. In 1518, Antonio Sangallo the Elder was commissioned by the Florentines to design the pilgrimage church of San Biago. This was the second-largest church project of its time after St. Peter's in Rome. It is one of the most spectacular churches in Italy, built of travertine in a honey color that blends with the wheat fields. The building is in complete harmony with the landscape as well as the people of the area. Locate a deli and find a scenic, comfortable spot for your picnic. Use your imagination for prepared deli foods in the showcases and don't forget the wine and bottle opener!

In the Wheat Fields of Pienza

Pienza is one of my favorite towns in the Val d'Orcia of Tuscany, not only because of its spectacular views of the countryside but also because of its superior examples of the renaissance – a great location for a picnic.

The Piccolomini family took possession of the territory in 1458. Enea Silvio Piccolomini was born in Pienza and later became a pope, taking the name Pio II. Restoration began under his direction and remarkable architectural churches such as the Church of San Francesco and the Palazzo Piccolomini were constructed. If you plan on a visit to Italy, you must visit Pienza, not only for its monuments but also for the pecorino cheese. If you're not in the mood for a picnic, try the Trattoria Latte di Luna on the Via S. Carlo for a lunch or dinner *alfresco* where you can order the pappardelle with porcini mushrooms.

The author in Pienza cheese shop.

Other locations:

Overlooking Florence in the Hills of Fiesoli

On the Stradi di Vino in the Chianti Valley

On the lawn next to the Leaning Tower of Pisa

In the park in Rapallo overlooking the boats in the harbor

In the picnic groves at the Michaelangelo Hotel in Chianciano Terme\

At the top of Pitiliagno on a grassy area as you enter the ancient town

Glossary

Abbastanza – enough
Acciughe – anchovy
Affare – affairs
Aficionados – friends
Agita – indigestion
Amici – friends
Anguilla – eels
Antichiassimo – antiquity
Appassionato – passionate
Aragosta – lobster
Asparagi - asparagus

Baccala – dried salt cod
Bacio – kiss
Bara – coffin
Barone - baron
Benedizione – benediction
Bravo – clever; well done
Brodo – broth
Bugia – lie

Cacciatore – hunter
Cacciucco – couscous
Campagna – country
Campestre – rural; rustic
Cannelloni – white beans
Cante - singing
Cappelletti – pasta
Carne – meat
Carnivale – carnival
Cavolo –cabbage
Ceci – chick pea

Chiesa – church
Chiudere gli occhi – closed eyes
Colazione – breakfast
Compare – godfather
Compleanno - tip
Coniglio – rabbit
Coperta –blanket
Cozze – mussels
Creaturi - creatures

Cucina - kitchen
Cugini - cousins
Cura – cure

Delizioso – delicious
Disgrazia – disgrace

Dissimile – different
Dolce fare niente – sweet doing nothing

Farcito – stuffed
Farfalle – bow-tie shaped pasta
Figlio mio – my brother
Filetti – fillets
Finocchio – fennel
Formaggio – cheese
Fossetta – dimple
Frenesia – frenzy
Fritatta – omelette
Fritelle – pancakes
Fungi – mushrooms

Gallina – chicken; hen
Gamberetti – shrimp
Gamberi – lobster
Generale – general
Giorno – day
Granchio – crab
Grazie – thank you
Gustoso – pleasant

Imbottire – to stuff
Incontro – meeting

Libro – book
Limoncello – A lemon liqour
Limone – lemons
Lo no normale, vecchio – I am not normal;
I'm old
Lumache - snails

Maiale –pig; pork
Male – sick
Mangia - eat
Mangiafagiioli – bean eater
Marito – husband

119

Melanzane - eggplant
Mercato – market
Mervavigliosa – marvelous
Mio babbo – my father
Miracolo – miracle
Mistura – mixture
Moglia – wife

Nasone grande – large nose
Nipoto – grandson
Nonna – grandmother
Nonno – grandfather

Occupato – occupied
Ogni giorno – every day
Oratore con autorita – authority with
audience
Orgoglioso – proud

Paisano - countryman
Paese – country
Pancetta – Italian bacon
Pappardelle – wide, flat pasta
Paradisio – paradise
Parla – speak
Parla la siempre – always talking
Pasta fagioli – bean soup
Patati - potatoes
Pesce – fish
Polpette – meatballs or croquettes
Pomodoro - tomato
Posta – post office
Prigioniero – prisoner

Quaresima – Lent

Riprene – take back
Ritirarsi – retired
Romanza – romance
Rumoroso – noisy
Rustico – rustic

Sacriligio – sacreligious
Sagras –festivals
Salmone – salmon
Salsa di crema – cream sauce

Salsiccia – sausage
Salute – health
Saporito – tasty
Scarola –
Scherzo – joke
Scoppio – explosion
Scusa – excuse me
Secondo – second
'sfortunato – unfortunately
Sgombro – mackerel
Sincero – sincerely
Slealta – disloyal one
Sogliole – sole
Sorpressa – surprise
Specialte piatto – special plate
Splendido – splendid
Statista –statesman
Stomaco acida – acid stomach
Straccio – rags
Stradinario – extraordinary
Strega – a dark yellow, strong liquor
Subito – quick

Tagliarini –
Tonno – tuna
Trasferrire – transferred
Trattoria – inn; restaurant
Ufficiale – official
Umbriaco – drunk

Vescovo – bishop
Viglia di natale – Christmas eve
Vitalizio – for life
Vino nobile –
Vivere – to live
Vongoli – clams

Zafferano – saffron
Zio – uncle
Zitto – silent
Zucca – pumpkin
Zuppa – soup

About the Author

Donato Fortebraccio—educator, investor, writer, food critic, and cook *straodinario*, has always been known for his outspoken comments on the preparation of food, service, and restaurants in general. He was approved for membership in the international platform association, founded by Daniel Webster in 1831, as the American Lyceum Association. Such famous writers and personalities as Lowell Thomas, Jack Anderson, Art Linkletter, Victor Borge, and ambassador Enrique Tejera-Paris were on the membership committee. He is also in who's who in contemporary authors.

One of his writings, *My Godfather's Recipe Book* was reviewed in house beautiful magazine as well as numerous other media.

He enjoys annual visits to the peasant hill towns of Italy and is passionate about its food, wine, and people. Donato's compare Giovanni and his mother Maria instilled in him the love of everything (ogni cosa) about the art and secrets of preparing Italian food. A graduate of Boston area schools he presently resides in Naples, Florida, summers in Maine and can been seen visiting trattorias, restaurants, and wineries on the back roads of Tuscany with his wife Arlene .